UNITED
The Busby Era

UNITED
The Busby Era

Mike Prestage

DB PUBLISHING

First published in Great Britain in 2002 by The Breedon Books Publishing Company Limited, Breedon House, 3 The Parker Centre, Derby, DE21 4SZ.

Paperback edition published in Great Britain in 2012 by The Derby Books Publishing Company Limited, 3 The Parker Centre, Derby, DE21 4SZ.

ISBN 978-1-78091-148-9

Printed and bound by CPI Group (UK) Ltd, Croydon, CRO 4YY

Contents

Acknowledgments

To all the ex-players and long-time supporters of Manchester United Football Club who took the time to share their memories, with special thanks to Sir Bobby Charlton, Johnny Morris, John Anderson, John Doherty, Ian Greaves, Albert Scanlon and David Sadler.

Introduction

MANCHESTER UNITED can rightly claim to be one of the world's biggest and most successful clubs in both financial terms and on-the-field success. Yet the foundations of today's triumphs were laid in the post-war years when the club took as their manager a man who would lay claim to being the greatest manager in English soccer history. For the best part of a quarter of a century Sir Matt Busby was the guiding hand at Old Trafford.

Of course, the roll of honour achieved by Manchester United under the tutelage of Sir Alex Ferguson is a magnificent one and in some quarters the seemingly heretical is being considered by some of the club's supporters that the manager has eclipsed his legendary predecessor.

Yet there are many of a certain age for whom the sides created by Busby hold special memories. Particularly as the post-war years were a remarkable era for football as crowds flocked to grounds in numbers never seen before or since. After the austerity of the war years people wanted entertainment and football was the leisure escape of the masses. While the crowds flocking to Premiership matches nowadays may seem large they are a shadow of the numbers heading for football grounds across the nation after the war.

The standard of football was also very good. The maximum wage ensured no players earned more than £12 a week during the season and £10 in summer. There was therefore little incentive to move and many teams were packed with local-born players. Talented individuals like Tom Finney at Preston North End and Nat Lofthouse at Bolton Wanderers were happy to spend their entire careers at their local clubs. It ensured quality was spread perhaps a little wider than in the modern era.

Yet as football returned after the war Manchester United were not in the healthiest of conditions. The financial problems that had plagued the club in the 1930s were still not completely resolved. And the Old Trafford ground had been severely damaged in a German air raid in March 1941 with the main stand largely destroyed and the pitch scorched. Until 1949 United would play home games at Manchester City's Maine Road ground.

When League football returned the fixture list abandoned seven years earlier was dusted off and as though having been frozen in time the matches were played again. There were a few faces from before the war years with the United captain Johnny Carey having made his debut against Southampton in September 1937.

One player happy to be back playing football was John Anderson, who had been with the A team as a 16-year-old, but whose career was interrupted when war broke out. He had been recommended to Manchester United by his former school master. A Salford-born lad, he was joined in the A side by Charlie Mitten, Stan Pearson, Johnny Aston, Johnny Morris and Allenby Chilton.

As he explained: "We were all lucky enough to survive the war and returned from active service having lost six years of our playing careers. The players who had been in the A team with me would form the nucleus of the post-war team. It was wonderful to be back playing football and there was a sense of making up for lost time."

He had played some wartime football and remembers being up against Stanley Matthews who was playing for Stoke City. He must have turned in a good display because Walter Crickmer, the United secretary, paid him £2 instead of the usual £1 10s. He also had his first meeting with Matt Busby, who he was dropped to make way for because Matthews was turning out for United and it was felt a more experienced right-half was needed to give him the service he demanded.

The life of a footballer in the early years of Busby's tenure was a far cry from the lifestyle those pulling on the red jersey enjoy today. Anderson's first wages at Old Trafford when he returned after the war were £5 a week, which rose to £8 if he played in the first team with a £2 win bonus and a £1 for a draw. "The club was in dire straits financially in that first season after the war and there was hardly enough gear for everybody. I remember using my Navy jersey as part of my training gear. Tracksuits were non-existent though Busby banned the use of tracksuit bottoms because he claimed they restricted leg movement."

Training was hard as players strove to regain match fitness after being away so long. Anderson still has far from fond memories of those early sessions under the strict control of coach Jimmy Murphy. "Some days we could hardly walk home. We were training mornings and afternoons Monday to Friday."

They were, though, good times to be a professional footballer. As

Anderson and many players of his generation say there was something about this era that brings back memories of sportsmanship and fair play that appear to have been lost to the modern game. Though make no mistake there were many hard and uncompromising players about. This is a time that pre-dates satellite television coverage, corporate hospitality and players living the millionaire lifestyles of Hollywood film stars. There was little time either for the histrionics indulged in by today's players.

Many players relate tales of travelling with the fans on public transport to training and home matches. And if the team lost there would be no shortage of terrace experts ready to tell them where it had all gone wrong on the journey home. The maximum wage meant the players were close to the fans in more than just travel arrangements. Their lifestyles were little better. Not just in the 1940s, but through into the 1960s as well, although times were beginning to change then as David Sadler for one recalls.

He was an England amateur international with Maidstone United when he opted to turn professional with Manchester United, although there was competition from Spurs, West Ham and Arsenal. He arrived at just the right moment as this was the time at which the maximum wage was abolished and he started as a professional on £20 a week, which shortly before would have been the most the top players could earn.

He recalls: "It seemed fantastic money. I had started work in a bank on £5 a week so it was a huge rise for a lad just turned 17. I'd never really travelled much from the little village I was brought up in, so being in Manchester was a new experience. Given this was the 1960s and the city was at the hub of all that was happening it was a great time to be there."

United fanatic Annette Kelly remembers, though, that even in the 1960s the players were accessible for the fans. "I had a photograph I cherished for years that I took of George Best and the goalkeeper Pat Dunne standing at a bus stop waiting for the bus back home. A few of the players had cars, but not all of them."

Another anecdote involves her husband Mike, who had gone to Oldham Athletic to watch a testimonial game. "I used to go and watch the players train in the school holidays and a couple of us had gone to watch the game at Oldham. After the match we chatted to Maurice Setters and asked him for a lift back to Manchester and he gave us a lift. Can you imagine that happening today?"

When football resumed in the 1940s, though, a young football fanatic couldn't get enough of the game. Bobby Charlton would go on, of course, to be one of the great legends of not only Manchester United, but also the world football stage, and receive a knighthood. Indeed, there was a time in the late 1960s and early 1970s with the boom of the package travel industry that in tourist resorts across Europe the names "Manchester United" and "Bobby Charlton" would often be the only common language with the locals.

He remembers as a child an era long before package holidays. He recalls: "There had been the war and for many people life was still hard and it was a great release to go to a football match and enjoy the game. The crowds were there in their droves. It was an exciting period to be playing football. There were also some great players about like Stanley Matthews and Tom Finney."

He echoes a question often asked by many players who plied their trade in the 1940s and 1950s. "One of the things that sometimes makes me wonder is given the grounds were full and the clubs never paid big money with the maximum wage in force where did all the money go?" It is a question unlikely ever to be properly answered.

A player who would play a key role for United in the Busby Babes side of the 1950s was Albert Scanlon and, as a lad growing up in Manchester, he recalls that it was City who were the more famous of the local sides and, like most of his contemporaries, he was a Sky Blues fan. After all, he remarks, United didn't even have a ground of their own.

When he arrived at Old Trafford he was surprised by the size of the playing staff at the club. The maximum wage meant big squads of players. When he became a professional in 1952 he was one of five outside-lefts. It meant a tough battle for the coveted first-team jersey.

"Many were old-time professionals who had been away for the war and there were also a lot of part-timers," he says. "It was the same at other clubs and when we played Central League matches you had to be careful. We were kids playing against seasoned professionals and I quickly learned not to dwell on the ball because someone would give you a kick. It certainly toughened me up and provided valuable experience."

Also, he recalls the life lacked the glamour enjoyed by the modern player. "Nobody had a car. We all travelled by bus with everybody else. As far as I remember Matt Busby had the only car. Because many of us were young and had come through youth football together we often shared the same digs and used to socialise together. United was a very close-knit clan of players."

Scanlon recalls that when he signed on the ground staff at Old Trafford as a 15-year-old, he was earning 15s 6d (78p) a week, which may not sound a lot but was more than his father was earning working in a tyre factory. In his own career, he reflects, he was at the right club, at the right time and with the right people around.

What rankles with Scanlon, and many other players, was the way there was no shortage of officials with tickets for the gravy train that was football in his day. He remembers: "I was playing for the Football League against the Irish League in Bangor, County Down, and as I came back from a walk a coach pulled up and a crowd in suits and ties and carrying briefcases all got out. They were Football League officials and there were 52 of them. After the match we were all on early flights home and it was the officials who went to the official banquet. That's how it was."

Manchester United always had a famed scouting network and inside-forward Johnny Morris, who hailed from the Lancashire mill town of Radcliffe, was spotted by one of the club's most famous scouting figures Louis Rocca. He left school at 14 and after a successful trial at Old Trafford was taken on the following year for the £10 signing on fee.

Yet Morris, a critic of the often murky world of football in those days and a firm believer that the players didn't get a good deal, recalls that his own arrival at Old Trafford was not so simple. A teacher at school had recommended him to his local club, Bury. Yet the manager there, Norman Bullock, advised Manchester United that he had talent.

Morris says: "Why the manager of Bury should recommend me to United I'll never know. Nor will it ever be known if money changed hands. It certainly seemed strange at the time and more so when I look back on it now. That, though, led to my trial and at 15 I signed as an amateur while still working in a paper bag factory. It was 1938 and just before the war."

While the money players earned in the 1940s pales in comparison with the salaries today's stars earn, Johnny Morris echoes the view that, compared with the ordinary man in the street, United's footballers were well paid and it ensured a good lifestyle. Manchester United provided his first house at a rent of £2 a week, which was not cheap but it had the advantage of not being far from the ground, and a couple of the other players lived nearby.

He remembers: "Football was a good life and I enjoyed every minute of it. We trained from 10am until lunch time four days a week and the rest of the time was ours. On a Monday we played golf. Matt Busby loved his golf and so did I. It was an enjoyable day out. It certainly beat working in a paper bag factory which was my first job after leaving school."

Football was obviously vital to the players who made their living at the game, but it could also have far-reaching consequences for those who merely watched. Mike and Annette Kelly are lifelong fans and it was Manchester United who brought them together. Annette explained: "We both worked for the same company and were on a work's trip to Blackpool. I fancied him but the first question I asked was who did he support and when he said United, that was it. My boyfriend previously wasn't interested in football and he was useless." The two started going to matches together in the 1960s and, now happily married, they are still avid United fans.

Old Trafford was at the heart of a massive industrial complex next to the docks where the progress of fans could be delayed if there was a bridge swing. For young fan David Hollingworth, making his way to the ground for the first time on his own to see the last match of the season against Chelsea in 1955, it was the sights and sounds of the walk to the stadium and his first impressions in the ground that provoke more memories than the game itself. Many youngsters forced to quicken their pace to keep up with the throng of bodies heading for the match, and jumping the railway lines that crisscrossed the industrial park, will empathise.

Hollingworth, a United fan for the best part of 50 years and now an active member of the Rossendale Supporters Club, wasn't allowed to go to Maine Road with his father, who was a City supporter, because it was considered too dangerous and too far away. So he supported United and was finally allowed to make his way to the ground, which was four miles from their home in Salford.

He recalls: "Manchester was a sea of red brick, huge warehouses, factory and mill chimneys all smoking away even on a Saturday. Getting to the ground I negotiated the railway tracks with their little tank engines which pulled goods wagons literally alongside the stadium walls. The towering structure of the stadium seemed massive. On the open terrace of the Stretford End I was taken aback by the thousands of people. It was the start of a lifetime of support for Manchester United."

It was not just in travelling to the ground that players were more accessible. In those days the playing staff were happy to chat and sign autographs after training. Fan Ian Boswell recalls walking to Old Trafford from Stretford Grammar School during the lunch break to try and get players' autographs as they returned from training at The Cliff. "We were frequently in trouble at school for returning late from these trips."

As a youngster from Salford, Kevin Smith remembers the ritual that was Saturday afternoon as he made his way to the ground with his dad. "My dad would meet up with friends and they would go to the pub for a pint before the game and I would go to a café and then make my own way to the ground. In the Stretford End there was a great atmosphere and we all used to have rattles in those days. After the match I'd meet up with my dad and his pals. There was also the adventure of being taken to away games when we played the Lancashire teams like Burnley, Blackburn and Preston North End. Watching Manchester United was an important part of my childhood memories."

Manchester United have always attracted support from well beyond the city's boundaries and it was the case when Smith started watching, though the appeal of the club was not the same as its world-wide draw now when a trip to, say, Singapore can see locals walking down the road wearing their United shirts with pride. As a youngster the family moved to Rawtenstall in the heart of Burnley territory and he remembers the arguments at school were not always good natured.

"The Burnley chairman Bob Lord criticised United after the Munich tragedy and it provoked a huge row," he said. "That led to some heated exchanges at school, but once you are a United fan you never switch allegiances. As they do today, United can stir strong resentment among rival fans and that was particularly true of Burnley supporters."

Certainly Smith does not agree with the taunt often levelled at Manchester United that they have less support in the city than their rivals at Maine Road. He was born in Salford and it was his local team as it is for many others. But certainly he knows there is something special about the club. Its history, its success, the players it has attracted and the style of play have all added to the appeal of Manchester United.

Roy Collins, now 75, remembers that going to a football match was an important part of the weekend ritual for working men after the war. Like most he worked on Saturday mornings and then caught a train and bus from his home in Newton-le-Willows to the ground. "There wasn't much time to spare and I can remember some weeks I travelled to Old Trafford only to get caught by the swing bridge being opened and I'd miss the kick-off. There was nothing to rival football on a Saturday and the standard was good. There were so many stars knocking around and if the football wasn't as fast as it is today that's hardly surprising with those heavy boots and the heavy ball they used."

He looks back on his time following United as though the club were part of the family. "I've had a good life with a nice wife and children and a great football team to follow. I have really enjoyed myself with them and, though there might be times when you have the occasional fall out, you are still always together."

Many younger fans may be more interested in looking forward than taking a nostalgic trip back in time, and certainly wallowing in history at the expense of the present and future is not a good thing. Yet much of what is being achieved today flows from the legacy of the Matt Busby era. For fans old enough to remember, this is a chance to revisit a great time in the club's history. For those steeped in the modern era, it is an opportunity to gain a glimpse of what helped to make Manchester United such a force. As Collins remarks after more than 50 years watching the club: "Everything that happened in the Busby years is what has made Manchester United special today."

Sir Matt Busby

THE WAR was not yet over and Matt Busby would not be taking up his new managerial appointment until he was demobilised, but when the former Liverpool and Scotland player put pen to paper while still wearing his Sergeant Major Instructor uniform it was to transform the fortunes of Manchester United.

In close on 25 years at Old Trafford he would create three great sides and lay the foundations for the transformation of the club into one of the world's greats. There would also, of course, be the great tragedy of the Munich air crash. When Busby signed the contract and took on the £15-a-week United job, the watching club secretary Walter Crickmer could have had no idea what excellent value he was to prove. Busby even turned down a move to Tottenham Hotspur four years later, for what would have been a huge salary increase.

Having worked with Busby over nearly two decades, Bobby Charlton is well placed to give his verdict on the man. He says: "He was a great personality. He wasn't a coach as such and he never stopped and told you what to do. Generally the idea of tactics that are part of the game today, weren't part of the game then. What he did do was make sure he got the best players and then instilled in them a will to entertain. He stressed we must entertain. The people that came in to see us play had worked hard during the week and we provided their pleasure. His belief was that football should never be boring."

He acknowledges that there were great expectations on United to not only win, but to win well and it was up to Busby to make sure that not only did the youngsters keep coming through the well-honed system, but also if any good players with flair came on to the transfer market he had to go and get them, if they could aid the club. From Quixall to Cantona exciting players have been recruited to the Red Devils cause.

After Munich Busby, not surprisingly, became even less hands-on when it came to the team because he physically couldn't do it, according to Charlton. "After the disaster there was a different sort of approach and he relied on other people. But his dream of Europe was still there."

Busby himself always refused to be drawn on which of his three sides was the greatest. There was the post-war side of the 1940s; the Busby Babes who were on the verge of so much in the 1950s before the tragedy of Munich; and the 1960s team with which he would lift the European Cup. He had gained a great deal of satisfaction in putting them together and gained glory with each. As he often said, they were the best of their own time and comparisons between eras are irrelevant.

What was irrefutable is that he never swerved from his oft-stated dictum that United should always try and serve up a class of football of which the club could be proud. It was what marked out Manchester United as special, from when he began in the 1940s and throughout his reign. The Busby Babes were as famed for the way they played the game as for their results.

When pressed he would say his finest buy was Jimmy Delaney from Celtic for whom he paid £4,000 and who was sold to Aberdeen six years later for £3,000. As to the best player, there were too many contesting the title for him to commit himself, but clearly Duncan Edwards and George Best would not be far from his thoughts.

Busby's own playing career had started across the city at Maine Road and he played more than 200 games for United's great rivals before joining Liverpool for £8,000 in March 1936. While with Manchester City he collected a Cup winners and runners-up medal having played in the losing Final against Everton in 1933, and then being victorious against Portsmouth the following year. He played 125 games for Liverpool before war broke out.

Although still short of his 36th birthday when he took on the manager's job at United, there had been fierce competition for his signature. He had been offered a five-year contract as assistant to manager George Kay at Liverpool, and Reading and Ayr United were interested in offering him key roles. He had no hesitation though in returning to Manchester and filling a position that had been officially vacant since Scott Duncan left in 1937.

It's hard to believe today, but the club Busby took over was a long way from the Manchester United that was to stride across the European football stage during the 1950s and 1960s. The 1930s had been a difficult time with United close to financial ruin and saved only by the intervention of a last-minute benefactor who injected enough cash to pay the players' wages and strengthen the playing staff.

Between 1931 and 1936 they plied their trade in the Second

Division and their promotion as champions brought them football in the top flight for only one season before they suffered the ignominy of relegation. A year later they were back in Division One but only had one season before war intervened.

Busby's arrival was to spark a change in fortune and the results of his rebuilding were quickly to bear fruit. As we shall see in the coming chapters, Manchester United and success were to become synonymous during his long reign that would last until 1969. And even after then he returned for a year when his successor Wilf McGuinness was relieved of his post.

In his time at United he led the club to five League Championships, four FA Cup Finals, of which they emerged victors twice, and, on a glorious night at Wembley Stadium in 1968, a European Cup triumph that was the pinnacle of his glorious career. Only in the more recent reign of Sir Alex Ferguson have United enjoyed greater success.

Yet Charlton notes that it was not just in playing matters

Matt Busby, created not one but three great teams.

that Busby was astute. He also had a good eye for the commercial side of the game. Not content to just collect the money from fans pouring on to the terraces, he knew there was more that could be offered. Busby had visited one of the leading American stadiums and saw the good things they were doing to improve the spectacle for the fans and improve the commercial side of a club. Manchester United were one of the first clubs to introduce corporate boxes.

The impressive 65,000-seater stadium that is the modern Old Trafford, coupled with the huge commercial generating machine that is Manchester United is, Charlton believes, the legacy of what Busby first started in the early 1950s. And the money generated, unlike at some other clubs, is made available to ensure that, when they need to, the club can compete for the best players, and through the years they have done just that.

Yet in the early days Busby was very much a new recruit to the managerial role. He was not much older than his more senior players when he forged the 1940s side that was to dominate football in the post-war years, despite not having the services of the bomb-damaged Old Trafford. Enforcing his will was not always easy.

Johnny Morris recalls that while many remember Busby as a football elder statesman, when he first played under him he was not the figure of authority he would become. He had only signed a three-year contract and his long-term future was by no means secure.

An anecdote Morris relates shows how, in these early years, Busby relied on the experienced players in the post-war team. The 1948-49 season had started badly for the Reds and the team had lost its winning touch. Anxious to put matters right Busby called the first-team squad in for a meeting. As he watched the players file into the dressing-room Busby told them: "This will never do lads." Centre half Allenby Chilton agreed saying: "No, it's no good to us either because we are not getting our £2 win bonus." He then instructed Busby to sit in the corner and be quiet.

Morris recalls: "Allenby Chilton took over the meeting and you couldn't repeat the language he used to the players. The expletives were flying. It was a real clear-the-air meeting. The players knew what was needed without Busby telling them. John Carey was the official captain, but he was too nice a guy for the job. The real captain's job was done by Chilton. He was a strong character who made the team what it was. He'd take no argument from manager or fellow players. After that talk we went out the following day and beat Preston North End 6-1 at Deepdale, and with Tom Finney in their side, and we finished the season runners-up."

He believes the reason behind his decision to seek a transfer also highlights that, at this stage of his career, Busby was still a manger finding his feet in a new role. The records talk of the player's run-ins with Busby and cite the fact that he questioned some of Busby's tactics, but now more than half a century on, Morris has told of what really led to his departure from Old Trafford, and the subterfuge he had to undertake to ensure his departure.

He said: "Matt Busby was my golfing pal and after the Cup I said to him that I wanted my benefit, which was worth £750 for being five years as a professional. I had signed amateur forms at 15 and a professional contract when I was 17 and by 1948 I was nearly 24. United never treated the players right and, although Busby said I should leave it to him to sort out, a year later I had still not got my benefit. This time when he said he would sort it, I asked for a transfer.

"Busby's reply was straight and he told me 'While I am here you will never leave the club.' There were other players looking for transfers because we weren't getting a good deal at the club, but I was determined to get away because there was never going to be any money made at United. I had to think of a way of getting out. Unlike today you couldn't just demand a transfer. I won a big golf event for the staff and players at Old Trafford and received a medal and it dawned on me that because I was playing off a two-handicap, golf could be my way out. I went and saw the secretary Walter Crickmer and told him I wanted my cards because I was finished with football and wanted to be a professional golfer. They had to put me on the transfer list or they wouldn't have got any money for me."

He moved to Derby County for a British record fee of £24,500 in March 1949, and it is a measure of the poor deal that footballers of the era got that all he gained was membership to an exclusive golf club in the Derby area. Morris rejected a move to Liverpool because he was appalled that one of the directors guaranteed him a place in the England line-up at a forthcoming fixture if he signed for the club. "It hurt me that this director was an FA councillor and he was suggesting this was the way the England team was selected."

At Derby County he was selected for England on his own merits before later playing for Leicester City. Looking back, although he enjoyed greater glories with Manchester United ,he feels he was forced to leave because of the way they treated players and regards Derby as his favourite club. He does not though blame Busby.

He says: "He was a nice chap. Tactically I wouldn't put him in the top class, but he was a good bloke to play for. Remember as well, he was a rookie manager then. I used to play golf with him. I was just disappointed he never gave me a benefit. We used to play before crowds of 60 and 70,000 at Maine Road and that was a lot of money coming in. We never seemed to get any of it though."

Busby had chosen well in his choice of assistant. Welsh international wing-half Jimmy Murphy was the new manager's first signing and they would forge an effective partnership. They had met in Italy during the war, and Murphy became coach before, in 1955, being officially appointed assistant manager. In the aftermath of the Munich tragedy he held the reins at Old Trafford as Busby fought back from his horrific injuries.

Murphy had the chance to further his career away from Old Trafford, and was offered work in Brazil and with the leading Italian side Juventus, but he always stayed loyal to Busby and Manchester United. A shy man, he was always in the shadow of Busby, but those who were involved at the club never underestimated his role and the part he played in the creation of a great club. Busby himself always acknowledged his contribution and said the two complemented each other.

Matt Busby, accompanied by his wife and son, shows his CBE to photographers outside Buckingham Palace in July 1958.

It was also Murphy who did the bulk of the training with the players and it fell to him to guide the development of the procession of youngsters who would find fame as 'Busby Babes'.

This was a time when managers did not have such a hands-on approach with the players, though Busby spent more time in a tracksuit than most of his contemporaries. This was particularly so early in his managerial career.

Charlton believes it was the work of Murphy in his younger days that helped make him the player he developed into. He was often hard to work for but Charlton knows that there was good common sense behind everything he did. The training sessions with Murphy toughened him up for the life of a professional footballer and as he says, he owes him a great debt. Murphy resigned as assistant manager in 1971, but continued to scout for the club. He died on 14 November 1989, aged 79.

Like many at Old Trafford, Albert Scanlon recalls the unheralded, day-to-day work with the players which was done by Jimmy Murphy and Bert Whalley. Both had encyclopaedic knowledge of the teams they were due to face. On the mornings before home matches the team would meet at a local golf club and have lunch. After that it was just a case of going out and enjoying yourself as players, recalls Scanlon.

He had few dealings with Matt Busby. The manager might have a chat with the team on a Friday before a game and if there was anything that a player needed to sort out with the manager it was done via the captain, Allenby Chilton, who acted as a go-between. A role later taken on by Roger Byrne.

He said: "If you had any grievances you would go to the captain and say your piece and it was conveyed to the manager. If the boss had anything to say he would come and tell you. When I was younger I was just happy to be playing, but at United you always had to check the team sheet because no one was guaranteed a place. When I was older and expected first-team football, if I wasn't picked, I'd ask questions, but the reality was that you could either gripe and groan or get on with it and nine out of ten players just got on with it."

Another player whose first major influence on arriving at the club was Jimmy Murphy, was the young David Sadler. For Sadler his arrival in the early 1960s at Old Trafford was something of a culture shock, as he was now training and playing virtually every day and it was a tough transition from his amateur days, though he quickly got used to the new regime. At this stage Busby was not involved at all.

"Up until Munich, Matt had been pretty active in terms of training, but by the time I arrived we didn't see very much of him even when I made my debut and was in the first-team squad," he said. "As well as Jimmy Murphy, the people I saw on a regular day-to-day basis for training were Jack Crompton and John Aston senior. We would see Matt on a Friday and he would travel with us to matches. I was pretty much in awe of the guy when I first arrived. He already had the reputation as one of the top managers."

It was Murphy who would pull the young Sadler to one side to discuss the previous week's match and he was the man who discussed tactics, but there was no sense of players being overpowered by strategies. Neither before matches nor during the week were there much tactics talked. The old Busby creed still ruled, however the game might be developing elsewhere. "If the players weren't good enough they wouldn't be there and it was up to them to express themselves on the pitch," was his view.

Sadler recalls: "An hour or so before kick-off Busby would concede there was another team taking part in the match and would give us a run-down on the opposition. Only to make you a little bit aware. Otherwise it was a case of us going out and playing."

It was not unusual that the preparation of sides for matches was far from the science it is today though others were quicker to catch on to the new trends than United. Ian Greaves recalls, in his day Manchester United rarely talked tactics. Busby picked the side and they went out and played. It was the teams poorer in resources and playing power who relied more on giving themselves an edge through tactics and training methods. This was brought home to him when he saw the coaching staff of Bolton Wanderers going through their paces in the mid-1950s.

Greaves had begun his career with Buxton before joining United in May 1953. He was always on the periphery of the first team but his seven years at the club saw him play 75 first-team games and after the Munich tragedy he gained an FA Cup runners-up medal in the 1958 Final. It is as a manager he is better remembered, having been in charge at Bolton Wanderers, Oxford United and Wolverhampton Wanderers before becoming assistant at Hereford United. He ended his managerial career at Mansfield Town.

A day spent sharing training facilities with the Bolton players gave Greaves a rare insight into how another team prepares. The United players had the use of the pitches in the morning and Bolton were taking over for the afternoon session. What was revealed was a remarkable coaching session, which showed how well organised Bolton were for the time and how United were slow to catch on to modern training methods of the day. Though for all the science involved in the sport today, Greaves still believes the game is funda-mentally the same as when he played.

Greaves said: "I knew many of the Bolton lads and stayed behind to watch them train. All we were used to doing at Old Trafford was running around the pitch. We weren't given any footballs to use until the last ten minutes when we went and had a kick around at the back of the stand. This was the fabulous Manchester United training. When we watched Bolton we couldn't believe it. They were running and training with the ball at their feet, then kicking it up for others to head it. The training was organised and concentrated on skills. Within a few years everybody got in on the act. Bolton were ahead of their day on that score. It took the Hungarians to wake everybody else up when they came over and showed us we weren't the best in the world and had been complacent."

One great skill Busby did have was for identifying young talent and supplementing them by going out and buying the best around. Then as now money was no object for a club whose revenues could be guaranteed. Greaves once overheard a conversation in which a United director expressed his concern to Busby that the crowd numbers were down to only 52,000. This was when the Reserves could get 22,000 watching. United were buying players for £30,000 when local rivals like Wanderers, who Greaves would go on to manage, were looking to recruit from the lower divisions for £3,000.

Up and down the land football fans moan that Manchester United are able to buy success. Nowadays there are claims that the huge fortunes generated at Old Trafford and a handful of other Premiership rivals is to the detriment of today's game. Greaves has no sympathy and believes those critics miss the point. He reckons it was always the case. He points out Sir Alex Ferguson is doing the same as Busby did in making the most of the cash at his disposal. In his view people tend to have short memories.

Inevitably there has to be a ruthless steak to any successful manager. While he may care for the individual, the good of the club as he sees it must come first. For all players the time will arrive when their tenure at one of the world's leading clubs is at an end and that can be a painful business, as Albert Scanlon was to discover.

Busby could be brutal in his dealings with players of he decreed changes were needed. The decisions must have been hard for the manager and could cause lasting resentment in the player. One of the more difficult tasks must have been the decision to drop inside-left Scanlon in 1960, given the player had survived the Munich air crash with his manager.

Even today Scanlon says: "I didn't like the way it was done. Results hadn't been going well, but I'd scored in a 6-1 win against West Ham and we'd won the last two games I played in, against Newcastle and Forest, and when I found myself out of the side I knew I was on the way. Matt never said a word and I didn't argue with him. We were brought up like that at the club. It was hard for me because I had played the majority of the games since I came back after Munich. Matt was always ruthless."

When the end came for the player it was announced at a room in a hotel after a friendly game. Scanlon describes how John Aston came and told him the boss wanted to see him. They drove to the hotel and Busby was waiting. The manager told him: "I've accepted an offer from Newcastle United and it's up to you, but I think you should leave Manchester." When Scanlon said he didn't like the way things had been done Busby's answer was simply: "That's football."

However, other players had happier times with the great man. Busby was a powerful influence on Sadler, as the player is happy to acknowledge. He said: "Over the time I was to spend at Manchester United and, as I got to know him more and became closer to him personally, he became like a father figure. That was the way he was to all the young lads as they progressed. My mother passed away when I was young and my father died not long after I came to Manchester and he really did become like a father figure"

Given the swinging 1960s were dawning, Busby's paternal instincts also had to include keeping a close eye on young players in a city where there were a lot of attractions of a distinctly non-football nature. Given that Sadler was sharing digs with George Best, it does not need too much imagination to see the temptations yet, as Sadler recalls, the manager had what seemed a well-developed network of contacts in the city to keep him informed. There was a little rule book that all the young players were given with dos and don'ts, which included not being seen in town after Wednesday until after Saturday's match.

He remembers: "As a young lad all sorts of things happen. I was new to a big city. It wasn't necessarily a case of going off the rails, but there were attractions to a big city, including nightclubs. Yet it was incredible. He seemed to know every move almost before you made it. If you had been out late at a nightclub or in town having a few drinks, when you arrived for training the following day he would know all the details. You were called into his office and he put you straight, so to speak. There were a number of occasions I made the journey to the office to be told in no uncertain manner I was a professional footballer and shouldn't be doing these things."

John Doherty also recalls the encouragement he received from Jimmy Murphy in his early days at Old Trafford. "He was a nugget of a man, who loved his football. He was always tough, but if he thought you could play, and you got picked, he would always tell the player that he was as good as the rest. Given that United boasted some great players when I first arrived, that was great encouragement. You certainly weren't allowed any ready-made excuses about being 'only a kid.'"

As regards the manager, Doherty says Busby was exceptional. Once he had made his first-team debut he was put on full money and never earned less than that during his time at Old Trafford. He might not have been a regular choice but he still earned the same as the likes of Stan Pearson and John Carey.

Doherty says: "Busby was a good man who earned the respect of all the players. Being a manager is a difficult job and it is inevitable that you can't please everybody. Certainly there were times when I wasn't happy, but you just have to accept that. I stayed friendly with him and his family long after I'd finished playing football."

Busby was knighted following the European Cup win and was made a Freeman of the City of Manchester. He was a director at Old Trafford and then the club's President. He was elected a vice-president of the Football League in 1982. Busby died in January 1994. He was 84. On the news of his death fans arrived throughout the day to lay flowers and scarves beneath the Munich clock memorial and on the day of his funeral the procession stopped beside Old Trafford. Busby, the architect of the modern Manchester United, had gone but he had left the club in safe hands.

Close But Not Quite

I N THE first five seasons after the war Manchester United were League runners-up four times and the lowest position they finished was still a creditable fourth. There was no one side that dominated post-war football yet, try as they might, the team could never quite lift that elusive silverware. In their defence it should be remembered that it was not until 1949 that they returned to Old Trafford having played their home games until then at Maine Road.

The team that represented Manchester United at the resumption of football after the war provided a valuable foundation for the new manager and his new assistant, Jimmy Murphy, to build on. Certainly Murphy, years later, said the experience in the side gave Busby and himself the chance to seek out new players and plan for the future. It was also a wonderfully attacking side and that provided marvellous entertainment for the spectators.

For fans of a certain era the names of the players roll off the tongue with an ease born of many recitations. Personnel may have changed over the course of the four years, but the side best remembered is the one that took the field at Wembley in 1948: Crompton; Carey, Aston; Anderson, Chilton, Cockburn; Delaney, Morris, Rowley, Pearson, Mitten. They were the first of the three great sides forged by the manager.

John Anderson explains that teams rarely changed without good reason and when you got a chance in the first team you had to take it. Competition for places was fierce in a very competitive United side. In the first season after the war he played mainly in the Reserves before getting his break in the 1947-48 campaign. Fate played a big part as he willingly concedes.

"It was late December and I was travelling by train on the Friday to play a reserve game against Newcastle United," he recalls. "We had to change at York and there was an announcement came over the loud speaker asking for the trainer to report. Club captain Johnny Carey had been taken ill and I was to go back to Manchester to replace him. I made my debut against Middlesbrough and I had to mark Wilf Mannion, an England international and household name in those days.

"It was a wonderful moment to play my first game for the club and I had a pretty good match. We won 2-1 and it was like a fairytale for me. I was headline news in the papers with things like 'starts the day a reserve and finishes a star'. Carey was fit and back in the side, but then Joe Walton was injured so they moved Johnny to right-back and I was in. A good run of results and I was in the first team."

There was another bonus. Busby called him into the office and offered him a new contract as a first-team player, which meant his weekly wage rose to £12 during the season and £10 in the summer. "We were doing well in the League and at the end it was a disappointment not to have done better, but the highlight of course was the FA Cup run and a trip to Wembley."

Yet if Anderson was happy with the way the financial side of affairs was being managed one of his colleagues was not so enamoured. What rankles with Johnny Morris is that as League runners-up the players should have got a bonus, but they never got theirs. "Money was tight at Old Trafford and the players seemed to miss out. That was the way things were run. We only got a £20 bonus for winning the Cup Final when the match generated a fortune."

Manchester United line-up pictured in 1946-47, the first post-war Football League season, when United finished runners-up to Liverpool in a season that was extended until 26 May because of the severe winter. Back row (left to right): John Warner, Joe Walton, Cliff Collinson, John Hanlon (12th man), Billy McGlen, Henry Cockburn. Front row: Johnny Delaney, Johnny Morris, Jack Rowley, Stan Pearson, Charlie Mitten and Allenby Chilton. This was the side which drew 2-2 at Everton on 16 November, Pearson and Rowley scoring. Jack Rowley ended the season as United's leading League scorer with 26 goals.

After a loan spell with Bolton Wanderers and then two years in the Army in India, Morris returned from the forces keen to resume his Manchester United career. It was obvious competition for first-team places would be serious, with at least seven inside-forwards on United's books.

He says: "I had met up with Stan Pearson at various wartime games and when we returned we were both wondering what we would do. There was a bit of a nervous wait to see who would get in the side and both of us were unsure whether we would be in. In fact when I first got back I had gone and seen Matt Busby, who had been signed on as manager the previous year, and asked him if he would release me as a player given all the inside-forwards the club had.

Johnny Carey gets in the way of Arsenal winger Ian McPherson at Highbury in August 1948. United won 1-0 with a goal from Charlie Mitten, and that season finished runners-up.

"Stan was such a good player that he was in the first team straight away. Matt Busby asked me to come down and train and he would see how I did and within a fortnight I was in the first team and stayed there until I left in 1949."

Morris recalls that Busby bought a few Scottish players, but many of them didn't make the grade and ended up in the Reserves. He returned to the squad he had inherited and many of these players were local lads. It was a good side and everybody played their part in the team's success.

In this first season Busby allied the experience of the pre-war players like Stan Pearson, Charlie Mitten, Jack Rowell, Allenby Chilton and Johnny Carey with young players like Johnny Morris, John Aston and Joe Walton who had come through the Manchester United Junior Athletic Club. In the coming years the ability of the club to bring youngsters through the ranks at Old Trafford, and give them their chance earlier than many rival teams blooded their young players, was to be a hallmark of the Busby style of managing.

With the maximum wage clubs could afford to have large squads with many having professional A and B sides as well as a reserve team. There could be a wait of many years before a talented youngster got a taste of first-team action. That was not the case at Old Trafford where the mould was broken to such devastating effect. It was a measure of the strength of the young players Busby had inherited that while the first team finished the 1946-47 campaign as runners-up, the reserve side won the Central League.

Supporters could not have hoped for a better start as United won their first five games on the reel and enjoyed a 5-0 home victory over Liverpool that saw Pearson score a hat-trick. Inside-left Pearson was another local player who was born in Salford and joined the Reds from local soccer. He played before the war, making his League debut in 1937 as an 18-year-old. He played nearly 350 first-team games for the club before joining Bury in 1954 and ending his career at Chester where he was also manager.

In a season extended into June because of the bitter winter weather, Manchester United kept in contention. But on 3 May, a trip to Anfield to meet the League leaders was to effectively decide the League contest. The result was only 1-0 to Liverpool, but it was to provide a valuable breathing space for the eventual champions. United were back on the road the following week and managed a draw at Preston North End. A win over Portsmouth and a 6-2 drubbing of Sheffield United meant the season ended in a nailbiting finish. Liverpool, though, had a game in hand, which they duly won, along with their last match of the season, to take the title.

The United side had scored 95 goals during the League campaign with centre-forward Jack Rowley netting 26. Rowley had been on the books at Wolves, but was transferred to Bournemouth without playing a League game. United saw his potential, though, and paid £3,000 for his services and he made his debut in October 1937. He proved a sound investment playing more than 400 games for the club and winning six full caps for England. He left on a free transfer in 1957 and went to Plymouth Argyle as a player-manager. His managerial career saw him take charge at Oldham, Wrexham, Bradford and the Dutch side, Ajax.

The following season saw United again finishing as runners-up, but this campaign was overshadowed – in the eyes of the supporters at least – by the team's Cup run, which, as we shall see later, culminated in a trip to Wembley and a Final hailed by many as one of the best for the quality of the football. In the League there were some impressive results with two 6-2 victories against Charlton Athletic and Wolves in the lead up to Christmas. And the side tuned up nicely for their day at Wembley with a comprehensive 5-0 win over Chelsea the Saturday before. Yet in the end United were seven points behind Arsenal and only secured the runners-up spot on goal-average from Burnley with both sides on 52 points.

The 1948-49 season saw United reach the semi-finals of the Cup and only relinquish their hold on the trophy after a replay against Wolves. They were again runners-up in the League, finishing five points behind Portsmouth. Johnny Morris remembers: "We were playing well but could never manage to nick it. Given the squad we had, and that we were so close, it was disappointing that we couldn't get that Championship winners' medal and at the end of each season you can always look back and say 'if only' at various games, but it was not to be."

Manchester United's Charlie Mitten lobs the ball over Wolverhampton Wanderers goalkeeper Bert Williams to score his team's goal in the 1-1 FA Cup semi-final draw at Hillsborough in March 1949. Nearly 50,000 saw the game.

One of the more curious fixtures was a fifth-round FA Cup-tie that pitted the Reds against non-League Yeovil who had already acquired a reputation as giant-killers. On their sloping pitch the Somerset side had already accounted for Second Division Bury and, even more impressively, had then put out First Division Sunderland. Their performance had won the hearts of the footballing nation and, remarkably, there was a crowd of 81,565 to watch them face United at Maine Road. But any hopes of an upset were quickly dispelled as United ran out 8-0 winners with Rowley collecting five goals.

It had been eight years since United played at Old Trafford, but for the start of the 1949-50 season they were back. Although there was still work to be done and plans were in hand to improve the stadium, for the fans it was enough to be home. A shade under 42,000 made the journey for the opening fixture and long queues formed to get on to the terraces, ensuring that many fans missed the start.

The opponents were Bolton Wanderers and, although many of the United side had never played at Old Trafford, they were all happy to be there. The fans had the chance to cheer a home win with a 3-0 victory and the first goal at the reopened ground, falling to Charlie Mitten. The outside-left joined the club from school in 1936 and, though he made wartime appearances, he did not sign as a professional until 1945. He made his League debut with the resumption of football after the war.

Generally in football at this time, the tackles were harder but the spirit of the game was cleaner than in the modern era. Some might also say that the referees were more lenient in the 1940s and 1950s, which made an incident during the Reds' derby match with Manchester City at Old Trafford all the more unusual. Having been used to sharing grounds there might have been some camaraderie between the players, but there was certainly no fellowship between Henry Cockburn and City's winger Billy Linacre when they clashed in the closing minutes of a match the home side were winning 2-1. Both were sent off. Cockburn was visibly upset afterwards and was later to receive a seven-day suspension.

It was out of character for a player of Cockburn's quality and stature. Cockburn, at just 5ft 4ins tall, still managed to compete against bigger men to the extent that he won 13 England caps. The wing-half joined United from one of its nursery clubs, Goslings, and played wartime football for the club. He made 275 appearances before joining Bury in 1954 and later moved into non-League football.

A good early start to the season saw United go eight games without defeat until they went down 1-0 to Burnley at Turf Moor. The following week they suffered their first loss on their home turf losing 3-1 to Sunderland. But any hopes that the return to their own ground would provide the extra spark to take them beyond runners-up, and inspire them to finally win the title, were dashed with a disappointing run-in that saw only one win in the last ten League games, and that came in the last game of the season when Fulham were beaten 3-0. It ensured a fourth-place finish in the table, the worst since Busby had taken charge. In the FA Cup the Reds' interest lasted until the sixth round when a trip to Chelsea saw them go down 2-0.

The season also marked the

Referee J. H. Parker looks on as Wolverhampton Wanderers captain Billy Wright shakes hands with United captain Johnny Carey before the 1949 FA Cup semi-final replay at Goodison Park.

end of John Anderson's career at Manchester United. With the player already having lost his first-team place, he knew opportunities were going to be increasingly hard to come by. In October 1950 he left for Third Division Nottingham Forest for a £9,000 fee. The player received the £750 benefit because he had been with the club for five years and it helped him start a new life in Nottingham.

"I had a good time at United and was fortunate to play in a good side that played attractive football," he said. "I enjoyed my football career and had three years at Nottingham and then moved on to Peterborough. There weren't fortunes to be made in football in those days but it was a good life."

As the 1950-51 season opened, many of the players who had been

available to Busby when he first made the step into management were still in place. This season, though, injury was to account for one of the regulars. The goalkeeper Jack Crompton had played for nearly a month the previous season with a fractured wrist, but would make only two starts in this campaign. Crompton was another recruit from local side Goslings and was first-choice goalkeeper from the resumption of League football in 1946. He left United in 1956, but returned in a coaching role after the

Johnny Carey leads out United at Stamford Bridge in March 1950, for the FA Cup quarter-final tie which Chelsea won 2-0.

Munich disaster until Busby returned. He was back again doing a valuable backroom job when Tommy Docherty was in charge. As a player he appeared more than 200 times for United in League and Cup.

His place was taken by Reg Allen, who had been signed from Queens Park Rangers for £11,000. But another goalkeeper had arrived at the club who was to be the long-term successor. The one appearance he made, less than 24 hours after being signed from Darlington the previous season, was in a 1-1 draw against Newcastle United. It was, though, to give Ray Wood the distinction among many fans of being the first Babe given a first-team game. However, it was another season before the 'Babes' tag would be coined and, as we shall see, it would be in relation to two other key components of the Manchester United team that would form Busby's second great side.

Another player to be missing, but in more bizarre circumstances, at the start of the 1950-51 season was Mitten. During the close season he had joined a small group of players tempted to play in South America. In the days of the maximum wage the money on offer in

Colombia was too tempting and he joined a team called Santa Fé. Others making the journey across the Atlantic included Neil Franklin, the Stoke and England centre-half.

The club had travelled to South America for an end-of-season tour, which was where the offer was made. Busby warned of the difficulties for his career if he returned home because he faced suspension under League rules, but for a player now 29, and with a young family to support, the cash on offer was too attractive. Reports as to the package on offer varied, but it was said to include a £40 a week wage and a £2,500 signing on fee. A not inconsiderable sum at the time.

However, curiously the player himself does not appear to have consulted his family before making such a drastic career choice. The *Manchester Evening News,* in its reporting of the move at the time, carried an interview with his 29-year-old wife Betty back in Manchester where she appears incredulous that she would be heading for South America. "I am still going ahead with plans for a holiday in Scarborough in two weeks time," she is quoted as saying.

Sadly for the player and Betty, they were never able to settle and within a year he was back in Britain. There was no chance of a return to Manchester United, although he was still under contract. He was fined £250 by the FA and suspended for six months. When his playing career resumed it was with Fulham, before he moved into management with first Mansfield (as player-manager) and then, in 1958, at Newcastle United.

With the South American machinations behind them the rest of the team – many of whom had also been approached but had resisted the financial temptations of the Colombians – could concentrate on events on the field. With United's League form in three of the last four years being as runners-up there was a certain inevitability about the way things evolved. Suffice to say the Reds were to be the nearly men again.

Busby moved quickly to secure a replacement for Mitten and a good display in Bolton Wanderers' defeat of United brought to his attention Harry McShane. He was also unsettled at Burnden Park because he was competing with their England international Bobbie Langton for his favoured outside-left berth. In a cash-and-player deal he cost £4,500 and full-back Johnny Ball joined Wanderers.

The side, though, had an unsettled air about it. Busby used 23 players during the League programme as the old guard began to be replaced by younger blood and the manager and his coaching staff sought to find the right balance. In November the news broke that Busby's first signing Jimmy Delaney had been sold and was returning to his native Scotland to play out his career with Aberdeen. Delaney was bought for £4,000 in 1946 and sold four years later for £3,500. During that time he had played 183 games and won the affection of the crowd with his speed and ability on the wing.

Morris concurs with Busby's reputed view that his best signing was Delaney. "Matt Busby bought a good few players in his time and paid a lot more than he did for Jimmy, but I've always thought he was the best buy. He was brilliant to play with and was a Scottish international before he joined us."

In a bid to ring the changes, and in a move that proved inspired, Busby moved his full-back John Aston up to centre-forward as replacement for Jack Rowley who had 'flu. Although Aston had played in the forward line when he arrived at Old Trafford, it was as a full-back that he had made a first-team spot his own. Aston signed professional forms at the end of the war and won 17 England caps during a United career that spanned eight seasons before injury forced his retirement from the game.

The move worked as United made a storming finish to the season. On 13 January, after a three-match losing streak, they beat Tottenham Hotspur 2-0 at Old Trafford. Sixteen games later they drew a goal apiece with Blackpool and in that spell had suffered only one defeat, beaten by Stoke City, 2-0. There had been some comprehensive victories of which the biggest was a six-goal trouncing of Huddersfield Town with Aston and McShane, showing they had settled nicely into their forward roles, collecting two goals each.

It was a magnificent late rally but United could not overhaul Tottenham Hotspur who had led the table since January. There was also disappointment in the FA Cup where, having despatched Arsenal with a 1-0 home win to reach the sixth round, there was optimism among the players and on the terraces, only for United to be knocked out by Second Division Birmingham City with the only goal of the game being scored within 24 seconds of the kick-off.

Yet behind the scenes young players were beginning to force themselves into contention in the Reserves and junior teams. A few had been given the occasional outing in the first team. As yet the names of Mark Jones, Roger Byrne, Dennis Viollet and Jackie Blanchflower were known to only the keenest of United followers. It would not be long before they would attract a far wider following.

The Greatest Cup Final

I F THE League title continued to evade Manchester United there was at last to be the chance of glory and the first silverware of the Matt Busby era. The team battled their way to Wembley where they met Blackpool and produced a match regarded by many who saw it as the best the stadium had witnessed. Too often Cup Finals can be an anti-climax as nerves take their toll. This was not the case in 1948.

The route to the Final had been a tough one for United. They faced First Division opposition in every round and en route accounted for the League Champions Liverpool and the Cup holders Charlton Athletic. It was a measure of the side's goal scoring prowess that their six Cup games saw 22 goals scored. Eight of those fell to Stan Pearson, the inside-forward who had signed for the club in 1937.

For their opening match the opponents were Aston Villa and United travelled to Villa Park for what proved a thrilling encounter. They were a goal down after 13 seconds but were leading 5-1 by half-time. A late rally by Villa gave the home crowd hope and at 5-4 United could have fallen at the first hurdle until a late goal by Pearson sealed the match. It was gripping stuff.

After the Villa game Johnny Morris recalls: "It was one of the most exciting games I have played in and afterwards we knew we would win the Cup even though it was only the first round. Although we conceded a goal early on we didn't panic and everything just came right. That day was

Johnny Morris shoots for goal during the 1948 FA Cup quarter-final 'home' match against Preston North End, which was played at Maine Road. A crowd of over 74,000 saw United win with goals from Pearson (2), Rowley and Mitten.

the best I remember the side playing. Everybody was on top form. Some of the lads who liked a bet were telling fans they knew to get their money on us while we were 25-1. It was said one supporter got £1,000 on. We had such a good team it was unbelievable."

John Anderson also has fond memories, having only just established himself in the team, although the opening few seconds caused him a moment's concern. Goalkeeper Jack Crompton was the first United player to touch the ball when he picked it out of the net, and Anderson remembers looking up at the clock in the corner of the ground and seeing the hands still firmly pointing to two o'clock. Not the best start he has enjoyed in a football match, by any means.

The problems of sharing their home matches with Manchester City were to become apparent during the Cup run. For the next round the Red Devils – always Busby's preferred moniker for his teams rather than Babes – secured a home draw against Liverpool, but found that City had a home tie on the same date. It meant a trip to Liverpool but to the Goodison Park ground of Everton rather than Anfield. In front of a 74,000 crowd they duly despatched the Merseysiders with a comfortable 3-0 win.

There followed another home draw, another fixture clash and again a desperate search for a venue. The opponents were Charlton Athletic and the venue was Leeds Road, Huddersfield. Anderson missed the game having been injured the previous week in a League game but he recalls: "We were having the best of it and putting them under a lot of pressure." A goal in each half was enough to settle proceedings and United were comfortably through to the next round.

Next up were Preston North End who boasted the indomitable Tom Finney in their ranks. However, not even the presence of one of England's greatest forwards of all time could stop United's relentless march to Wembley as they ran out 4-1 winners with the chance to play this home tie at their preferred venue of Maine Road.

United went all out for attack and it paid off as the Preston defenders struggled to prevent a glut of goals being scored. It was a tough baptism for the North End goalkeeper Jack Hindle who was making his first-team debut. The visiting fans, who had made the short journey to ensure a crowd of 74,243 was shoehorned into the ground, reluctantly had to concede that the four goals United did score was not an unduly flattering result.

Anderson has particularly poignant memories of this match because his wife, who had been suffering from TB, had died the week before. He remembers the help and support he received from the club and Matt Busby during his wife's illness. Her funeral was the day before the Preston game and the decision on whether to play or not was left to the player, although the manager's view was that life had to go on. Anderson agreed and recalls he did not have a bad game.

The semi-final draw pitted United against Derby County, with the match to be played at the Hillsborough Stadium in Sheffield, while Blackpool would take on Second Division opposition when they met Tottenham at Villa Park. Applications for more than 30,000 tickets flooded into the Old Trafford office where officials had just 19,700 to distribute ranging in price from two shillings and sixpence (2½p) up to the most expensive stand tickets at a pound.

The match itself was an open contest early on, but United struck on 30 minutes when Pearson took advantage of some hesitation in the Derby defence to meet a Jack Rowley cross. Four minutes later Pearson scored again, taking advantage of a mistake by the Derby goalkeeper Jock Wallace to head his second with the provider this time being Jimmy Delaney. A fine goal by Billy Steel just before half-time kept Derby in contention, but the last word went to United's inside-left who collected his hat-trick and booked United's ticket to Wembley with a goal early in the second period.

Many United fans had taken advantage of odds of 25/1 at the start of the competition and the fervour that had built with each successive round was now at fever pitch. The club had been besieged with ticket demands for each round and the intensity of the demand could not be quenched. Given Blackpool were the opponents and their line-up would include the legends Stanley Matthews and Stan Mortensen, this was going to be a Final to savour.

Team page from the 1948 FA Cup semi-final programme against Derby County at Hillsborough. United won 3-1 with Stan Pearson getting a hat-trick.

United had not been to a Cup Final for nearly 40 years and it was the first time in the Seasiders' history that they had gone this far. While the football club was concentrating on the job in hand on the field, the town of Blackpool was looking to enhance its reputation as a leading tourist attraction. In many ways they were ahead of their times in viewing a major sporting event as a valuable marketing opportunity for more than just the club.

The approach, though, perhaps lacked the finesse of modern marketing strategies. One suggestion was for hats decked out in the football club's colours to be distributed with the words "Blackpool is a holiday winner" emblazoned across them. Then, as now, the town was not backward in pushing the name of Blackpool forward. Such an approach has helped ensure that the seaside resort is still a major holiday destination, just as it was in the 1940s.

With demand far outstripping supply at both clubs it was manna from heaven for the ticket touts who were offering to buy 3s (15p) Wembley tickets from season ticket holders as they collected them, for £3 each. There were reports of the black market price for four stand tickets being £50. A small fortune when the average weekly wage was around £6. United had received more than 30,000 applications for the 13,500 tickets allocated to Old Trafford.

Morris remembers that the night before the Final a few of the players were sitting around in the hotel when Charlie Mitten ordered a round of rum and blacks to celebrate getting to Wembley. Drinking alcohol before the big day was strictly against the rules.

He added: "I was teetotal at the time and so were a couple of the others but the rest all took the drinks. Everybody was surprised that Charlie had done it and they hid the drinks under the table so that Matt Busby or any of the directors wouldn't see them. Afterwards players were putting the drinks down to helping us win the Cup, but the manager would have been furious if he had known."

United fans in good heart, pictured in Trafalgar Square before the 1948 FA Cup Final against Blackpool at Wembley.

Generally he recalls that everybody was relaxed before the game. Although there was the excitement of the occasion most of the players did not suffer from nerves. With the exception of Anderson. "He had a pre-match routine of sneaking to the toilet for a Woodbine. You could smell the smoke. I'm sure he would have done the same at Wembley to calm himself," says Morris.

Anderson's own Wembley build-up had seemed to involve just about everyone he had served with in the Navy during the war writing to ask for a ticket and a good few he's certain he never met. The player also had his own anxious moments with his place by no means certain. He was relatively inexperienced and Busby had the choice of using Jack Warner instead. Happily he opted for Anderson who recalls: "Playing in a Cup Final at Wembley is every player's dream and I was going to be there. It had been a difficult time for me personally and I was going to enjoy this day."

There had been some dispute over the money the players were to receive for appearing in the Final. Unlike their modern contemporaries players had little negotiating power with their clubs and there was not the chance to exploit the appearance at Wembley with media interviews and marketing or promotional opportunities. The club had decided that each player would receive only a £20 bonus for reaching the Final. Given the income the match would generate the players were justifiably aggrieved. The refusal of the media to make any payment resulted in the players covering their faces as they left the train station en route to the team hotel to prepare for the match.

Just has United had done, their opponents remained in their home town and kept to their routine as best as possible. They did, though, in the week before the Final, travel to nearby Lytham to practice on the grassy promenade that was reckoned to be the nearest thing to the lush Wembley turf. For all but the three internationals, Matthews, Mortensen and Harry Johnston, it would be the players' first visit to Wembley. In the days before the Final the team stayed at a hotel in Ascot and used the facilities at Royal Wentworth Golf Club for training.

Skipper Johnny Carey introduces United's team to King George VI.

With Blackpool the opposition, all the fans were heading south and the Lancashire dialect could be heard everywhere. Fans of the Seasiders wearing tangerine and white hats and huge rosettes sat on the lions beneath Nelson's Column and tried to create more noise with their rattles than the Manchester supporters who had taken up station beneath Admiralty Arch with chants and cheers for their side. There was great rivalry but it was good natured, very much in the spirit of the age.

To try to cut down on pre-match nerves the Blackpool team planned to arrive as near to the kick-off as possible. The teams were expected to be there at least an hour before, but the Seasiders were determined to be at the stadium certainly no sooner than that. The view of Stan Mortensen was that the team that settled first and forgot it was Wembley but just another football match would win the game.

Once the teams had been presented to the King and Queen, two of the most skilful sides in English football, both with a reputation for playing attractive football, prepared to do battle. The game itself lived up to all expectations and even today is still talked of as one of the greatest Finals for the football that was produced. For the Blackpool fans the trophy would not be coming back with them to the coastal town. The final score of 4-2 to Manchester United flattered the winners, but there could be few complaints about the result against a side that just had the edge.

With the clash in colours both sides wore a change strip. Blackpool took to the field in white while United were in blue. With two minutes gone Matthews fashioned an excellent shot for Alec Munro who mishit the shot from close range. In the 14th minute, though, it was Blackpool who took the lead. Mortensen was brought down on the edge of the penalty box and the referee pointed to the spot. It was

Charlie Mitten gets in between Blackpool goal-keeper Joe Robinson and full-back Eddie Shimwell.

a controversial decision with United players and fans claiming the foul was outside the penalty area. Undeterred, Eddie Shimwell showed that the practice he put in during the week before the match was not wasted and duly converted the kick.

Allenby Chilton was a rock in the United defence but Morris remembers: "He had a habit of making one silly mistake in a game and sure enough it happened at Wembley when he fouled Mortensen in the box and conceded the penalty. Even though the challenge looked worse than it was, the spot-kick was still given. At least the error had happened early on and after that Chilton produced a flawless display."

United had devised a tactic to try and negate the influence of the legendary Matthews. Morris explained how, to keep the great man quiet, Mitten at outside-left was instructed to drop back a little way and stay closer to Matthews to make it difficult for the Blackpool players to pass to him. It was, he believes, a key factor in United winning the Cup.

Perhaps spurred by a sense of injustice at the goal, United came storming back. The pressure brought its reward when, in the 30th minute, 'keeper Joe Robinson and Eric Hayward dallied when a Delaney cross came over, and Jack Rowley took advantage of the momentary lapse to equalise for the Reds. Seven minutes later Mortensen had achieved the rare feat of scoring in every round of the FA Cup when he got on the end of a Matthews free-kick. Blackpool still had the lead at half-time.

In the second period Blackpool were far from overawed and Matthews was creating chances, although the Manchester defenders were coping well with his crosses. Hopes that the lead could be increased were dashed when Hugh Kelly was penalised for handball. A quick free-kick by Morris saw Rowley again capitalise on a mix-up between Robinson and Hayward. With ten minutes remaining United were having the better of it, but Blackpool still had their chances. Now Anderson made a long pass to Pearson whose 25-yard shot beat Robinson.

Minutes later the Cup was secure for Manchester when a shot by Anderson found the net. Anderson was the unlikeliest of scorers and 50 years on he recalls the goal that was the highlight of his career. "I pushed the ball past a player coming to tackle me and looked to pass, but there was no one there unmarked so I took it on and then let fly with a shot and fell over. I never even saw the ball go in the net I just heard the roar of the crowd and knew we had won the Cup."

Morris recalls his role in the key second goal for United that brought the teams level. "We got a free-kick which I took and put it on Rowley's head and it was in. When we won it was a very emotional moment. It was brilliant going up to receive the medal. We shook hands with the Blackpool players. I played alongside Matthews in games for the English League. He was always the crowd pleaser. Wherever he was playing there was always an extra 10,000 on the gate just wanting to see him. Winning the Cup Final, though, was definitely the highlight of my soccer career."

Hugh Kelly, the Scotland international and Blackpool's wing-half, recalls: "It was a great game with open football. We were beaten, but up until halfway through the second half everybody was enjoying it and we were still in with a chance. They were worthy winners in the end. At the time we didn't realise what a good game it was, but later the fans were talking about it being one of the best matches seen. Certainly both teams walked off knowing they had played their best and I thought I had a good game. When I used to see supporters in the town later I told them we had all played well and done our best."

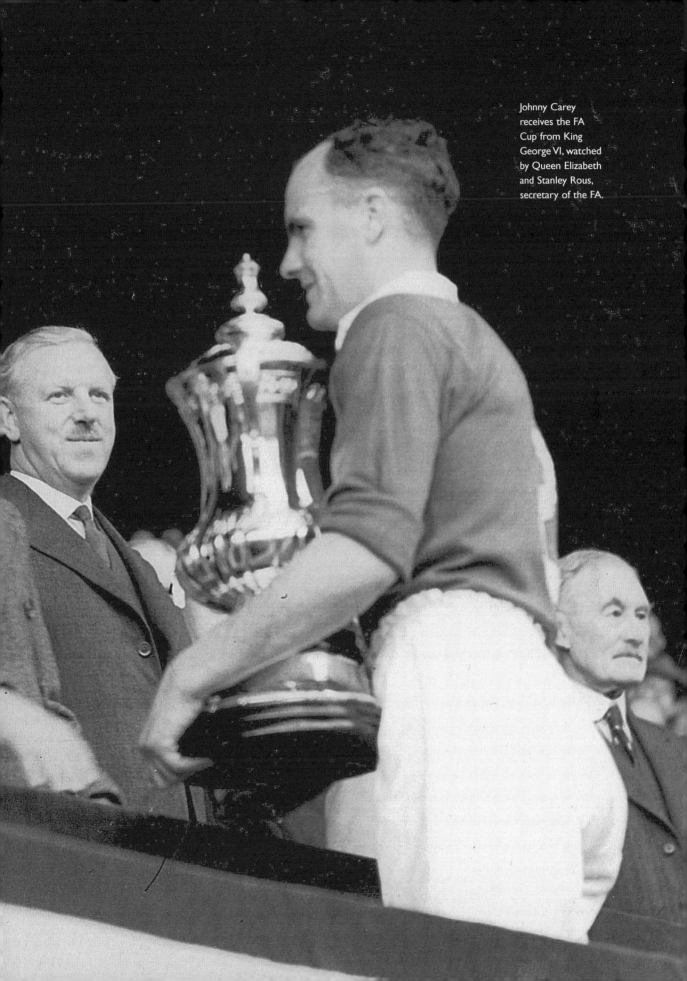

Johnny Carey receives the FA Cup from King George VI, watched by Queen Elizabeth and Stanley Rous, secretary of the FA.

Blackpool supporter Peter Collins had been lucky. Someone he knew had acquired a ticket and then at the 11th hour was unable to go and he was the beneficiary. He travelled down on the train and soaked up the atmosphere. He says: "Perhaps surprisingly I don't think I was ever worried about us winning or losing. The fact that we had got to Wembley and I was travelling to the big city to watch the Final was enough for me. Such was my faith in Blackpool at that time, and the view I had that we were the top team, there was an attitude that if we didn't win it this time there would soon be another chance. It proved to be such a good game of football and really exciting that,

Jack Crompton is beaten by Eddie Shimwell's penalty-kick at Wembley.

although we lost, I thoroughly enjoyed the day."

In the aftermath of the Final, Blackpool manager Joe Smith said that he thought that, with 20 minutes to go and the team still winning, the Cup was theirs. But Smith knew the fortunes of football could change quickly and so it proved. He was proud of his players and the performance they had put in and also the way they had been magnanimous in defeat. At the dinner at the Mayfair Hotel in London that night the view echoed time and again was that it was a match that would be remembered by all who saw it. Johnston, the Blackpool captain, said the team had done their best and the Manchester United team had deserved their win. Busby admitted: "We'd nearly given it up when you were still in front with only 20 minutes to go."

For the United players there was a banquet that evening at the Connaught Rooms and then the following day the party travelled to Brighton. On the Monday they returned to Manchester and the inevitable heroes' welcome and the coach made its way to the Town Hall where the players stood on the balcony and held aloft the Cup. On the Wednesday they had a League game against their Cup Final opponents at Bloomfield Road. Mortensen got the only goal but it was poor consolation for the vanquished Finalists.

Champions at Last

AFTER being so close so often this was the season when Manchester United were finally crowned champions for the first time since 1911, with a team that included a backbone of players who had served Matt Busby well since he first took charge, but with a smattering of the young bloods who would carry on the success story through the 1950s.

1951-52 was also the season when a new word came into vogue in the press to describe the talented young players being thrust into the limelight. When United had failed to gain a win in the first three games in November, Busby decided to ring the changes for a visit to Anfield on 24 November. Thus, Liverpool were the first opponents that 18-year-old half-back Jackie Blanchflower and full-back Roger Byrne, 22, faced in the top flight. Suddenly newspapers began talking about "Babes".

Manchester-born Byrne would go on to be an inspirational captain for United until his life was brutally cut short in the Munich air disaster. Yet at one stage in his early career he was not considered good enough for the RAF team. Another quirk was that although right-footed, he established himself in the left-back position. When Busby tried to move him elsewhere, he asked for a transfer and the manager backed down, returning him to where he was happiest. It was a rare example of a player winning a showdown with the boss.

Byrne is also credited with being the first of the modern full-backs, as it was he who developed the idea of making overlapping runs to support the forwards. Given that Busby had hoped to move him to the wing, Byrne had all the skills necessary, allied to a keen football brain, to make the innovation work. He won 33 consecutive caps for England and was expected to captain the side in the 1958 World Cup finals, but fate decreed that was not to be.

United made a sprightly start to the season, going the first four games without defeat before, on 1 September, they faced Bolton Wanderers at Burnden Park. It is not a new phenomenon that the presence of the Red Devils can raise the game of the opposition. Resentment at the club's success, its financial resources and the fact it represents one of the highlights of the season for players and spectators alike all play their part. In the 1950s that was particularly true of the small town rivals in industrial Lancashire.

However much money Manchester United might have generated in whichever decade, at the start of the 1950s the Bolton fans must have been reaching for their lucky charms because they seemed to have a jinx on their illustrious neighbours. Both sides were unbeaten and it was the visitors whose run was to end. The only goal came courtesy of England centre-forward Nat Lofthouse, who after being played onside by a United player was happy to make the most of the opportunity. A Willie Moir cross had taken a deflection. Attempts by United players to get the referee to consult a linesman and overturn the decision fell on deaf ears, to the relief of the home fans.

Chances were few and far between with the defenders of both sides having the upper hand, but United were to rue two good chances wasted by Jack Rowley. When Bolton targeted teams that could pack Burnden, United were top of the list and that was confirmed with a 55,477 attendance that set a new post-war League record for the ground.

Busby was full of praise for the consistency of his side over the seasons since he took over and early in this campaign he was already beginning to believe that the Championship trophy might finally be coming to Old Trafford. His experienced players were performing well – Rowley had scored three hat-tricks in the first seven games of the season in a total of 14 goals – and he was confident the new players he might have to introduce could do the job. He was proved right.

Yet while the League campaign was on course, in the FA Cup there was one of those setbacks that make the competition so special. The visitors to Old Trafford for the third-round tie were Hull City, who were lying second to bottom of the Second Division. United fielded a full-strength side, went 1-0 down after four minutes, missed a penalty and then saw the decisive winning goal conceded just before half-time for an ignominious defeat. In modern times a manager might mouth platitudes along the lines of now being able to concentrate on the League, but in the 1950s for United's players it was embarrassing and for the fans a shocker.

However, whether not having the distraction of a Cup run helped or hindered is a matter of conjecture. What certainly cheered the fans was that a fortnight after the Hull City debacle the terraces were able to cheer the return of an old favourite whose career had been troubled by injury. And a derby game against Manchester City was the best possible stage for John Aston to get back into action.

Back in the business of League football such blips as that suffered against Hull City were few, though back-to-back defeats against Huddersfield Town and Portsmouth in the last week of March and first week of April made sure the run-in to the title would be a close contest. And as John Carey was to reflect at the end of the season, Cup upsets can and do happen which is why players always value the Championship as the most important. The team that lifts the trophy has earned it by being consistently the best.

With five matches remaining United, Arsenal and Portsmouth each had 48 points. It began that most beloved pastime of supporters that involves checking the fixture lists and playing the 'what if' game. Certainly the fans could reflect that the Reds' fate was in their own hands and one match in particular was already setting the terraces talking. On the last day of the season the visitors to Old Trafford would be Arsenal for a possible Championship decider.

In the run-in the only point dropped was a drawn game away at Blackpool and there were some comprehensive wins to boost confidence as everyone at Old Trafford sensed this was to be their year. Liverpool suffered a 4-0 defeat at United and the visitors the following week, Burnley, fared worse going down 6-1. In the penultimate game Chelsea were beaten 3-0 and the stage was set for Arsenal although results elsewhere had ensured the game was going to be an occasion for celebration rather than a nail-biter.

For the mathematicians Arsenal were still in with a shout. For the rest it was over. The Gunners needed to win by seven goals. There were that many, but six of them were scored by the Red Devils to emphatically claim their Championship. In fairness to Arsenal they were down to nine men at the end, losing first outside-left Don Roper after 25 minutes and then centre-half Arthur Shaw with four minutes to go, both injured in the days before substitutions were allowed.

Rowley opened the scoring after eight minutes when he got on the end of a long pass forward by John Carey, and two goals in a minute just before half-time settled proceedings. Rowley finished with a hat-trick and a tally for the season of 30. It had been a marvellous all-round achievement by United and a thoroughly deserved reward for the consistency they had shown since the war.

Captain John Carey knew he had won his coveted medal with his career at Old Trafford drawing to a close and it was true of others. There had been five players in the Championship-winning side who had played alongside him at Wembley in the 1948 Final. For Allenby

Chilton, Henry Cockburn, Stan Pearson, Jack Rowley and John Aston time was also running out.

Carey was one of the great figures at Old Trafford both before and after the war. He had joined United from his native Dublin in 1936 with a £250 fee being paid to local side St James' Gate and within a year was not only in the first team at Old Trafford but had won the first of his caps for the Republic of Ireland. Legend has it that the scout Louis Rocca had crossed the Irish Sea to look at another player, but when he saw the young Carey he quickly snapped him up.

Originally an inside-forward, after the war he moved to right-back where he played for seven years, although in his long career he played in every position except outside-left having even gone in goal from the start in a match against Sunderland in February 1953 when Ray Wood was ruled out. He made nearly 350 League and Cup appearances for United and his stature in the game was recognised when he was made Footballer of the Year in 1949.

When he retired in 1953, as a mark of their appreciation, the United directors invited him to a meeting of the board so that they could personally thank him. He went into management with spells at Blackburn Rovers (twice) Everton, Leyton Orient and Nottingham Forest.

His successor as captain was another Old Trafford legend who would prove a valuable and experienced player alongside the new Babes coming through the ranks as he bridged the gap from the post-war side to the new Busby Babes team that was set to dominate the 1950s.

Allenby Chilton was the powerful centre-half at the heart of the Manchester United defence in nearly 400 games for the club. Keen fan John Prestage recalls that as a youngster it seemed that, while Busby was keen on flair and innovation elsewhere in the side, at centre-half he liked an old-fashioned rugged player who relied on strength. Chilton was one of the best of such a breed.

Originally from County Durham he had joined Liverpool as an amateur in 1938, but moved to United later in the year after failing to make the first team at Anfield. His League debut was against Charlton Athletic at The Valley on 2 September 1939. A date memorable because it marked the last fixture before the League programme was suspended for the war.

He was back in the side when football resumed, which meant his second League game had come seven years after his debut. Chilton won two caps for England and was an ever-present in the United side until he surrendered his place to Mark Jones. A measure of his durability is that his last League match against Wolves in February 1955 marked the end of a four-year run of 166 League games without missing a single match.

When he left he took on the role of player-manager at Grimsby Town in the Third Division (North). He finished playing for the Mariners in 1956, after winning them promotion, but continued as manager for another three years before moving to Wigan Athletic and later Hartlepool United.

Many of the team who had played in the 1948 Cup Final and won the 1952 Championship were already gone by the time Bobby Charlton arrived, but he caught the end of the United careers of Chilton and Rowley. "When I was in the juniors we would play on a Saturday morning and then go and stand in the crowd to watch the first team. We felt it was a real bonus that we got in free and could go and stand in the Paddock."

Other regular first-team players were now finding themselves in the Reserves where Charlton got to meet them and learn a lot from them. Players like the goalkeeper Jack Crompton and Henry Cockburn gave the young Charlton good advice and he was always prepared to listen.

Albert Scanlon was another of the young players waiting in the wings but he remembers the jubilation at the club that the title had at last been secured. "Having come so close so often it was fitting that some of the great side of the 1940s had finally got a Championship-winning medal. It was no more than they deserved and a fine tribute to their efforts that had laid the basis for all that was to come at Old Trafford."

A New Team is Born

MANCHESTER United had won the title but now it was time for Matt Busby to ring the changes and, for many of the old guard who had served him well, a Championship medal was to be the final reward before moving on, their places taken by young players waiting in the wings.

The purchase the previous season of the Cliff training ground meant there were excellent facilities for United's junior teams to train and play. In the Championship-winning season, a portent of the future was provided in an FA Youth Cup fixture when United beat Nantwich 23-0, with five goals by Duncan Edwards, five from David Pegg and a goal for Albert Scanlon.

Scanlon, whose uncle Charlie Mitten was in the great United forward line of 1948, had turned professional at the club in 1952. Having played for Manchester Boys while still at school, he was invited for a trial by United and recalls there must have been lots of others who had hoped to get their chance yet he was the lucky one on the night and was invited down to the club.

He said: "The competition was fierce just to get accepted. You might see 40 or 50 lads one night and then you'd only see one or two of them again. People think the Busby Babes were started in the 1950s, but the process was under way by the 1940s. I worked at the ground and you could see the huge numbers of young players coming and going as the club trawled for the best talent. When I was first there I didn't train with the senior players. The young players did our own training and the rest of the time I cleaned boots, swept and did odd jobs."

When United started its youth team, Scanlon was a key part and he played in the 1953 and 1954 FA Youth Cup-winning teams. The bulk of those he played alongside would go on to form the backbone of the Busby Babes side. Even then, he recalls, they were an impressive side. "I remember that Nantwich game and there were 10,000 there watching and we won 23-0. That was the sort of interest we were starting to generate even as youngsters." A secret of Busby's success was his willingness to nurture young talent, coupled with the knowledge that when he needed a player he was not afraid to spend heavily to secure his services. It was an irresistible combination that produced teams capable of fulfilling his philosophy of playing attractive, attacking football that the public would happily pay to watch.

The nursery for his Babes built on the work done before the war by the Manchester United Junior Athletic Club. Talented coaches were entrusted with developing the youngsters and an effective scouting operation was put in place to scour the home nations and Ireland for the stars of the future. Nothing was left to chance, including the selection of landladies who would provide a comfortable, homely environment for the young players and help overcome any sense of homesickness. Soon it would pay dividends.

As a young player arriving in 1953, Sir Bobby Charlton remembers being at Old Trafford was particularly exciting because Busby was already establishing his reputation for playing youngsters. The era of the Busby Babes had just dawned. And as a player he felt that if he was good enough, he would get his chance.

"I was 16 when I arrived and already Busby was showing his willingness to give young players a chance in the first team, which was unheard of," he says. "The general view was that it was a man's game and was not for young players. It was an exciting time and I think the quality of the game was improving. There was much more emphasis on coaching. As Busby proved his idea worked other teams started to learn."

The opening to the 1952-53 season was not the stuff of Champions. United won only one of their opening five games and it was apparent that an era had come to an end. It was a mark of the transitional nature of the season that 30 players would be used during the campaign. Many would become household names and grace not just Old Trafford, but the international stage. Two in particular would enter the pantheon of legends. Both Duncan Edwards and Tommy Taylor made their United debuts.

While there might have been discontent among some of the more demanding fans Busby himself was not worried at the early League results though he was aware of the task to rebuild his side. He is reported to have told the annual meeting of Manchester United shareholders at this time that the young players on the club's books represented assets worth hundreds of thousands of pounds who would soon provide the material to keep the Reds at the very top of the British game.

Yet on the terraces one young fan remembers that the idea of bringing in young players was not universally popular at first. Although in time it was to prove the making of the club, and Busby would be hailed as a great innovator, John Prestage found himself listening to older supporters making clear their discontent.

He recalls: "At that time teams didn't change much. You pretty well knew who would be playing each week barring injury. Many of the old guard that Busby was gradually replacing with the youngsters were firm favourites with the crowd. They had brought the club success during the 1940s and people identified with them as much as with the club. There used to be great debates on the terraces about whether dropping the old players was a good idea. Once the Babes starting winning matches though the fans were quickly won over to Busby's way of thinking."

Certainly Busby went about operating as he believed was right. He broke the bank to pay the club's highest fee for a player, and the second-highest in League history, to ensure the signature of Barnsley inside-forward Tommy Taylor on a Manchester United contract. There were rumoured to be 17 other clubs in contention but the player himself made clear his preference was for United. Busby paid £29,999 to ensure Taylor was not saddled with the burden of being a '£30,000 signing'. Incidentally, the British record fee had been set at £34,500 with Sheffield Wednesday's signing of Jackie Sewell of Notts County in March 1951.

Eddie Lewis scores one of United's five goals in the FA Cup fourth-round replay against Walthamstow Avenue at Highbury in February 1953.

On 4 April, and barely a year after his successes in the Youth team, Duncan Edwards was switched from his duties as a junior with the ground staff to make his debut in a 4-1 home defeat by Cardiff City. The result and United's progress in the League and Cup that season were barely worthy of note – eighth in the League and a fifth-round defeat at the hands of Everton after an earlier hiccup when they needed a replay to beat non-League amateurs Walthamstow Avenue – but the arrival of Edwards was to earn more than a footnote in United's history.

Among the other Busby Babes to be given their chance this season were David Pegg, Bill Foulkes and Dennis Viollet. Another making his first appearance was John Doherty, who believes he was the last youngster to be spotted and sent to Old Trafford by the legendary scout Louis Rocca when he was still a schoolboy playing for Manchester Boys. Although he was a City fan, it was United who showed early interest along with Leeds United.

United goalkeeper Ray Wood punches the ball off the head of Everton's Dave Hickson and up into the air at Goodison Park in February 1953. The Merseysiders won this fifth-round FA Cup-tie 2-1 in front of almost 78,000 spectators.

Doherty recalls: "Leeds United talked about ensuring I could continue my education, but when you are a young player that is the last thing you want to hear. All I wanted was to play football and be told by people how they could make me a professional footballer. I arrived as a 15-year-old in the 1949-50 season and began working in the office. It was something I never dreamed would happen. It was remarkable. Here was I training with the likes of Carey, Pearson, Rowley and Delaney. This was a team that had won the Cup in 1948 and was regarded as the best team in the country."

A home game against Middlesbrough on 6 December 1952, saw Doherty make his first-team debut along with David Pegg. Doherty remembers his selection was made public on the Friday and, to protect him from any media attention, he stayed the night at the home of coach Jimmy Murphy. A run of poor results had persuaded Busby to give the youngsters their chance.

"It was a great experience and a big change to go and play at that level. Just lining up alongside those players was special. I can't remember much about the game as the excitement and adrenaline took over. But I know we won 3-2 and Stan Pearson got a couple. That season was one of transition and a lot of new players got their chance and some of the old hands were coming to the end of their playing careers. We might not have earned anything like today's play-ers, but I'm sure we had more fun."

As a first-team player he joined the squad on a special training trip to Scarborough where they stayed at a top hotel and played some golf as well as getting some training done. "It was brilliant staying at the

September 1953 and United's Jack Rowley is challenged by Spurs and England right-back Alf Ramsey. Rowley scored United's goal in a 1-1 draw before 52,837 fans at White Hart Lane.

hotel with the senior players. That's when I thought I'd arrived. I was there with all the big stars. That weekend we travelled to Chelsea and I scored two goals in a 3-2 win and we had John Carey in goal for part of the time after the goalkeeper Jack Crompton had his jaw broken by the England international Roy Bentley. In the first three games I played we scored eight goals and won them all. People were starting to take notice. The idea of the Busby Babes was being talked about and there was a feeling this was the start of something special."

That January he played his first derby game with the Reds gaining a 1-1 draw at Old Trafford and Doherty reveals that for him the games were no more important than any other. "It sounds daft but for the players it was just another game. The importance of the match to the fans is far greater and they place a lot more on the results. Certainly I don't remember any antagonism between the players, but to be honest in those days the fans got on pretty well. They all travelled together on the buses and went for a pint together. Nobody then would have believed the day would come when fans had to be segregated at football matches."

There was, though, to be disappointment. Busby said he was giving him a rest although Doherty, like all professional footballers, just wanted to be playing and felt disappointed to be dropped. There was worse to come when he picked up a knee injury playing against Brentford in the semi-final of the FA Youth Cup.

He recalls: "Eddie Lewis and I ran from the ground after the game to get to the old Longford Cinema in Stretford. I can even remember the film. It was *The Road to Bali*. The film finished, the anthem was played and the lights went up and I couldn't get up because my knee had locked. I was doing National Service in the RAF but contacted Jimmy Murphy who told me to get to Old Trafford. I needed a long operation on what started as a cartilage injury, but finished as a knee operation. In comparison with today's standards the medical treatment was a form of legalised butchery. I had no sooner got over that then I had another injury on the same knee. I always had massive problems with it and I was never as good a player again."

John Carey had retired in May and for the new 1953-54 season the role of captain was shared between Stan Pearson and Allenby Chilton. It was not the best of starts. On the field United managed to go eight games without a win before a trip to Middlesbrough gave them the chance to break their duck with a 4-1 win. Results still did not improve greatly and so Busby finally decided drastic changes were needed.

Some commentators and United aficionados believe the defining moment – when the great era of the side forged in the post-war years ended and the new Busby Babes who would dominate the 1950s before the fateful night of the Munich air disaster began – can be highlighted with just one game; an away match to Huddersfield Town on 31 October 1953. The result was a 0-0 draw, but that is of no consequence. The significance of that game was that there were seven players no older than 22. Many had played before but this was the first time the Babes formed the bulk of the team.

Skipper Roger Byrne runs out at Highbury.

Results in the second half of the season improved, although there was a 5-3 reverse against Burnley in the third round of the Cup which ensured the young Babes would enjoy no Wembley glory this season. Certainly the performance ensured a fourth place in the League table. Not bad for a side going through such changes.

Also, encouragingly for United there appeared no end to the talent coming off the conveyor belt. In the FA Youth Cup the United side beat Wolves. Eight of this side would go on to play first-team football for United. They were also given their chance to shine in Europe when they were taken by Busby on a trip to Zurich to play in an international competition.

It is always considered a sign of a great manager that not only can he build a winning team, but he knows when to break it up and replace it with another. By the start of 1954-55 that process was virtually complete. It was of course often painful for those within the club and those on the terraces who had come to idolise particular players. Yet it was necessary and, although United finished fifth behind champions Chelsea, they were now poised to return to their glory days.

This was the season that Albert Scanlon made his League debut, following an appearance in a friendly against Hibernian, which United won 3-0. When the first team lost against Sheffield United the following week he was picked to play against Arsenal. 20 November 1954, is a date he will never forget. "I was very nervous and there were butterflies in the stomach. It was exciting and we won 2-1, but the following week we lost to West Brom and I was back out of the side. I got a good run towards the end of the season and in the end played 14 games."

He adds: "It was a time of transition. A lot of the older players were reaching the end and when I came back the following season many had gone and then I started wondering who was going to be in for the new campaign. I was always confident I would make it as a first-team player."

The changes being made did not always make for a happy changing room. Scanlon explained: "A lot of the older players were good ones and many had lost their best years to the war. Particularly at United there were a lot of youngsters coming through who were being given their chance and the older players could see what was going on. A lot of them naturally didn't like it. Jack Rowley played outside-left for a couple of matches and so I was competing with him for a place and he used to complain that I was too young. Before the war you had to be 25 or 26 to get in the first team, which was when Rowley started off. Busby changed all that."

Duncan Edwards, the prodigiously talented footballer.

It was a measure of how the young players were treated that Scanlon remembers he had to knock on the dressing-room door and wait for someone to shout for him to come in. He wouldn't think of arguing. "The older players were very proud and people like Allenby Chilton commanded respect."

In the FA Cup there was fourth-round defeat against neighbours Manchester City in a 2-0 reverse at Maine Road. Something never easy for the fans to swallow. But there was the satisfaction of doing the double over champions Chelsea. On the last game of the season United beat them 2-1 at Old Trafford, but that paled in comparison with the epic played out at Stamford Bridge the previous October. Then there were 11 goals in a remarkable match that saw United edge the victory by the one goal with Viollet scoring a hat-trick, Taylor scoring two and a goal from Blanchflower.

Tommy Taylor – 128 goals in 189 League and Cup games for United.

United had beaten the League champions but the following season they would achieve more than just the occasional memorable result. The players were in place and the scene was set for a return to the glory days that had been enjoyed by Busby with his post-war team.

Double Championship Winners

Top: Manchester City winger Jack Dyson leaves Bill Foulkes in his wake at Old Trafford but Mark Jones is coming across to get in a tackle. United won this September 1956 encounter 2-0 with goals from Whelan and Viollet. Bottom: Bill Whelan (8) scores for United, beating goal-keeper John Savage and Bill Leivers on the line.

MATT Busby did not have to wait long for his new side of Babes to show their pedigree. They dominated English football in the middle of the 1950s with successive Championship wins between 1955 and 1957 with players who, when they lifted the trophy for the first time, had an average age of only 22.

In 1955-56 they swept all before them, winning the title with two games of the season remaining and 11 points clear of Blackpool and Wolverhampton Wanderers, to establish an English First Division record. At a time when the League bristled with quality, United still managed to stand head and shoulders above the rest.

In the League, United quickly established their place at the top of the table and only three defeats from the dawn of the new year to the close of the season ensured they were never going to be overhauled. Pundits who wrote off the team at the start of the season, on the grounds of lack of experience, were made to look foolish.

Albert Scanlon recalls: "The press didn't give us much of a chance, but we soon made them eat their words. If anything, it made us all the more determined to prove our worth. We had a good side and were well aware of what we could achieve and we had the belief in ourselves not to be undermined by anything that appeared in the papers."

Yet with only two wins in the first five games, including a 1-0 defeat in the derby game at Manchester City, the early signs were not good. The Babes were talented for sure, agreed the experts of the day, and none would deny they were exciting to watch. But surely, they reasoned, this was a side for the future. Now though the team stepped up a gear and left the rest trailing in their wake.

Although dogged by injury, John Doherty battled his way back and in the 1955-56 Championship-winning season he began to win first-team selection. He recalls that Jackie Blanchflower's absence on international duty for Northern Ireland gave him an outing in a home match against Wolves. Doherty scored in a 4-3 win but a promise from Busby, that he would be given an extended run, didn't materialise as the returning Blanchflower went straight back into the side. Doherty did, though, play in 16 games in the season.

"I knew early on we would win the League that year, we had such a brilliant side," he recalls. "I had a spell out after taking a knock, but otherwise it was a great season. I won a Championship medal and went on the club tour to Sweden and Denmark. I thought I'd done enough to keep my place, but at the start of the next season I was left out. I was then at loggerheads with the manager. My argument with him was that if we didn't play well or lost it was always my bloody fault. I played just three games in the first team and was getting fed up."

With first-team opportunities scarce and further problems with the knee, Doherty's time at Old Trafford was running out, although he did receive a benefit. Jimmy Murphy told him there were teams interested and, out of the blue, Leicester City made an offer and he was glad to get away. He played just a dozen games before Leicester, against the advice of a Manchester specialist, decided to risk another knee operation, which brought his career to an end.

In the 1955-56 campaign Old Trafford was turned into a fortress with the home side unbeaten all season. It was thrilling stuff for the crowds who flocked on to the terraces and who had taken the new team to heart. Only two players from the 1951-52 Championship-winning side remained, in Roger Byrne and Johnny Berry, such was the overhaul that had taken place at the club.

One of the first to discover that Manchester United would be a force to be reckoned with were the League champions Chelsea, who visited Old Trafford on 19 November with the Red Devils already on top of the table. Now the press were beginning to doubt their earlier predictions and began talking-up the title hopes.

A week earlier, Eddie Colman, still doing his National Service in the Army, had made his debut. Colman caught the eye in this match as well and the 19-year-old quickly established himself as a favourite with the fans. The wing-half, whose trademark body-swerve earned him the nickname "Snake Hips", faced Chelsea's England international Roy Bentley, but that was not enough to daunt him as United ran out 3-0 winners. There were two goals for Tommy Taylor and one for Byrne. Both were already established internationals and would soon be joined by Duncan Edwards.

Colman was only 21 when he died at Munich but he had already established himself as an integral member of the Babes side. He had rapidly come through the junior ranks at Old Trafford and in his brief career managed more than 100 first-team appearances. He would surely have won England caps but for the tragedy, but his brief career still boasted two League Championship winners' medals and an FA Cup runners-up medal.

The first of his title medals would be clinched with victory over United's nearest rivals, Blackpool, when they visited on 7 April. The Seasiders were a great side, and with Stanley Matthews in their ranks they were a guaranteed crowd pleaser. Yet on this day the crowds did not need the draw of Matthews, nor indeed of former England legend Stan Mortensen, now nearing the end of his glorious Blackpool career, to have them flocking to the ground. The biggest crowd of the season – 62,277 – was crammed into the stadium with thousands more locked outside as the gates were closed half an hour before kick-off.

Blackpool, with their cast of internationals, were a major force in the 1950s, but they had never won the title and that ambition was not going to be realised on this day. United were aware of the importance of the game and broke with their usual routine. They travelled to an out-of-town training camp to prepare and keep the young players quarantined from the expectation that was building in the city. Busby recognised the excitement the match had generated throughout the North of England and acknowledged that Blackpool were a great side. He was, though, confident his side would win.

The Blackpool and Scotland international Hugh Kelly, looking back on that game, recalls that the Blackpool side took a positive attitude into the match: "The players were looking forward to the game and were confident. You have to approach such games in a positive state of mind. United had not been beaten at home all season but we thought if anybody could do it than it would be us."

The confidence proved misplaced against a side that oozed self-belief and also showed they could battle it out as well as produce some sublime football. An early strike for Dave Durie was not enough for Blackpool. Goals for Johnny Berry from the penalty spot and Taylor were enough to see United lift the title.

The penalty decision had been a controversial one. Blackpool players and fans felt the decision to penalise goalkeeper George Farm for a challenge on Doherty was harsh. There was also an incident when Bill Perry had a strong appeal for a spot-kick turned down when his legs were taken away from him. Few, though, could have complained about the final result with United always looking more dangerous in attack and their defenders more composed.

Kelly remembers: "The Busby Babes were all coming through. It was the first time I had seen Duncan Edwards. I had the ball in our own half right down in the corner. I had just reached it when this whirlwind arrived and it was Edwards. I thought "What the heck," and that was my first introduction to him and some of the other young up-and-coming United players. Sadly, in the case of Edwards and many of the others, they weren't around long enough for me to get better acquainted with them and their style of play because of the Munich disaster."

Manchester United players, 1957. Left to right: Ray Wood, Duncan Edwards, Tommy Taylor, Geoff Bent, Eddie Colman, Bill Foulkes, Jackie Blanchflower, Colin Webster, Dennis Viollet, Albert Scanlon, Johnny Berry.

A 1-0 victory over Portsmouth completed the season's programme and the crowds were again out lining the streets to cheer as the coach carried the victorious Championship-winning side to Manchester Town Hall, where a stage had been specially erected, and the players walked up to take their bow and hold the trophy aloft.

For one player, though, the 1955-56 Championship-winning season proved disappointing from a personal point of view. Having been selected in the first team, Albert Scanlon played only six games

Bobby Charlton, on the threshold of a great career.

before losing his position to his great rival David Pegg, who remained in the outside-left berth for the rest of the campaign. "Once I lost my place I knew there weren't going to be any changes because the team was on a roll. At that time you only needed two or three bad games and you were out, and it could be a long time before you got back such was the strength of the squad."

Pegg had played alongside Scanlon in the FA Youth Cup Final in 1953 playing inside-left, but he switched to outside-left at senior level and the two found themselves in competition. Pegg made his debut in December 1952 against Middlesbrough and made nearly 150 appearances for the club in six seasons having joined from playing for schools football in his native Doncaster. He won one international cap for England, but by the time of the Munich trip he had lost his place to Scanlon. He did, though, travel with the party and was fated not to return.

Tommy Taylor was the season's top goalscorer with 25 League goals and Dennis Viollet notched 20 in what had become a devastating forward partnership. There had been some impressive victories along the way, but also one shock. In the FA Cup third round United had travelled to Bristol Rovers, and their notorious mudbath of a pitch, and come badly unstuck in a remarkable Cup upset. They lost 4-0 to the Second Division side, underlining that the magic of the competition is its unpredictability.

Critics who had been sceptical before the start of the season were now prepared to accept that this was a side that could stay at the top for some considerable time. The club's record to this point, with two Championships, four runners-up spots and an FA Cup triumph in ten years of post-war football meant they could lay claim to being the pre-eminent side in English football. The success was to be repeated the following season.

Indeed, such was the talent of the side, and the ease with which they swept aside opposition, that the unthinkable in football was quickly starting to be regarded by many in the game as virtually a certainty: United would be the first team in the century to do the Double. With each round, the likelihood grew. The FA Cup can be an unpredictable competition and just one mistake can be fatal, so even the best can slip up. The Babes, though, made no mistake and booked a place at Wembley. However, as we shall see later, they were cruelly and cynically denied their place in history.

The remarkable pace set by the Babes in the previous season was maintained in the League right from the off in 1956-57. This was a side that had now added the experience of the previous year's campaign to its undoubted talent and few could stand in their way. The first 12 games saw them win ten and draw two. United were irresistible with 32 goals scored and 14 conceded. As with the modern Manchester United side letting them in never matters too much if you're scoring plenty more at the other end.

Pegg again retained the outside-left spot and Scanlon watched from the sidelines, playing only a handful of games as the season came to a close. He is, though, the first to praise the performances of his colleague. "David had such a good season. It is a measure of how well he was playing that when we played Real Madrid in Spain and though we lost they still went out and bought a full-back just to play the Old Trafford tie and counter the threat David posed. It isn't allowed now, but you could then add to your European Cup squad at any time. The whole team was playing some magnificent football and everyone was sitting up and taking notice."

It was not all good news though. The unbeaten sequence came to an end. After not losing on their home turf for all the previous season the impregnability of Old Trafford was now laid to rest in emphatic style against Everton who, on 20 October, scored five with the only consolation coming with goals for Bobby Charlton and Billy Whelan.

It barely slowed the Reds down, though, and the chasing pack never really got on terms. With Christmas and New Year behind them, United took to their task with relish and there were some veritable hammerings handed out. Newcastle United and Arsenal both made the long journey to Old Trafford and found the trip home seemed longer still after having six goals put past them. When United made their trip to London, Charlton Athletic suffered a 5-1 defeat. The occasion included a hat-trick for Bobby Charlton.

Coincidentally, Charlton made his first-team debut when the same team were the visitors to Old Trafford on 6 October, and he scored twice then. While many of his contemporaries got their chance early,

The Manchester United squad in the championship-winning season of 1956-57. Back row, (left to right): Colin Webster, Wilf McGuinness, Jackie Blanchflower, John Doherty, Eddie Colman. Middle: Tom Curry (trainer), Bill Foulkes, Bobby Charlton, Fred Goodwin, Ray Wood, Bill Whelan, Mark Jones, Duncan Edwards, Bill Inglis (assistant trainer). Front: Dennis Viollet, John Berry, Matt Busby (manager), Roger Byrne, Jimmy Murphy, Tommy Taylor, David Pegg.

Charlton served a long apprenticeship before he made the break-through. Though he never had any doubts that he would make it, he always knew it would be hard work and he would have to learn the trade of a professional footballer. It was, though, a life he badly wanted.

Charlton recalls: "I seemed to have to wait years to get a game in the first team. I had scored well in the Reserves, but while lots of other players were getting their opportunity I obviously wasn't quite ready. Matt Busby and Jimmy Murphy knew what they were doing."

He remembers being called in on the Friday before the team were due to play Charlton and, because he had picked up an injury, he was asked how his ankle was. When he assured Busby it was ok he was told he was in the first team. "I walked out thinking I had arrived. I was a professional footballer."

In what he describes as a "magic day" he scored two goals before a 41,000 Old Trafford crowd. "I was prepared and ready to take my chance. Playing at Old Trafford was the same then as now. It was the stage and there was an atmosphere I have never felt was at any other ground. The crowd is so close to the players. It is a unique place."

His other great memory of the season was his third game for the club when the opponents were Wolverhampton Wanderers, the pre-eminent team of the time though an honour that was about to pass to Manchester United. "Wolves were the team to beat and I learned a valuable lesson. It is not always the best team that wins. The team that wants to win the most and is prepared to push themselves that little bit further will triumph. Wolves were supposedly a better team and were well in front of us on points but, although they were a good side, we beat them 3-0."

A player Charlton singles out for helping him make the transition from reserve-team football to the first team was the centre-half Mark Jones. "He always had a lot of time for the younger players. He would be critical if you did badly but was always quick to encourage you when something was done well. He made me aware never to give the ball away because it is hard to get it back. There was a lot of pres-sure on the team and you quickly had to handle it."

Jones was another stopper centre-half in the manner of the player he replaced in the United side, Allenby Chilton. He was also another who came through United's junior ranks, having caught the eye as an England schoolboy international. Yorkshire-born, he made his debut in October 1950, in a 3-1 win over Sheffield Wednesday. He made 120 appearances for the club before losing his life in the Munich air disaster.

Tottenham Hotspur led the chasing pack for the title that included Preston North End and Blackpool, but when Sunderland visited on 20 April, and with three more games to play, the Championship trophy was retained. The crowd of nearly 60,000 saw a Manchester United team on the top of their game as they dismissed the challenge of the Wearsiders with ease in a 4-0 victory.

Billy Whelan scored twice with a goal apiece for Edwards and Taylor. Whelan edged Taylor in the season's goalscoring table with 26, in a campaign that saw United break the 100 goals barrier for the first time as they finished with a total of 103. Whelan was another player who would be a victim at Munich. He was born in Dublin and joined United in 1953 and succeeded in keeping Bobby Charlton away from the number-eight shirt as he amassed nearly 100 appearances in four seasons and scored 52 goals as well as being capped for the Republic of Ireland. For the fateful Red Star Belgrade game he had lost his place in the side to Charlton, but travelled with the squad.

United skipper Roger Byrne has just collected the Football League championship trophy. United were champions in successive seasons, 1955-56 and 1956-57, and were so close to an historic treble.

Manchester United had secured the League title and now had a date at Wembley in the FA Cup against Aston Villa. With the previous season's title earning a place in the fledgling European Cup, there was also the chance to gain honours on an international stage. This was a side at the height of its powers and, given the age of the players, the only question being asked was how much more they could go on to achieve.

Controversy at Wembley

MANCHESTER United's 1957 Wembley Final against Aston Villa was shrouded in controversy and even now, more than 40 years on, the incident that occurred in the opening minutes provokes strong feelings among fans of a certain age who remember how the dream of the Double was cynically ended.

Matt Busby himself said, later, that he had never been more confident of a victory in his footballing career. Neither he nor the massed ranks of United fans who had made the trip to Wembley could have predicted what was to happen.

The United goalkeeper Ray Wood had the ball in his hands and was preparing to kick upfield when he was flattened by Villa's Peter McParland. Wood's cheekbone was broken and he lay there dazed before being taken off. With him went the Red's hopes as Jackie Blanchflower took his place in goal and, in the age before substitutes, United were down to ten men. It was one of the most contentious acts in Cup Final history.

Bobby Charlton recalls: "I had got into the team for the semi-final due to injury and I didn't really expect to keep my place for the Final. I was really not expecting to be picked. We were going for the Double. It was unthinkable at the time. We had already won the League and we had a good team with a lot of internationals. Yet, at the time, every game was tough and there was no guarantee that you could beat anyone."

United were short-priced favourites, but, as Charlton reflects, losing the goalkeeper was disastrous. "For ten men to play at Wembley on a big occasion was always going to be hard. However, we still thought we could win. Tommy Taylor got a goal towards the end but, by that time, they had scored twice and it was too late. I had felt lucky to have played in the Final and while losing was disappointing, it was not the end of the world for Manchester United because we had so many good players and we were young and knew there was plenty of time ahead of us."

The Reds' route to the Final had given the fans the sense that this might be their year. The crucial slips that had blighted their Cup runs in recent years were put behind them. Certainly there was no repeat of the embarrassment of the previous year when they fell at the first hurdle to Bristol Rovers.

Although in their opening tie it proved a close-run thing as they edged Hartlepools United by the odd goal in a seven-goal thriller that had the small band of travelling fans fearing that the FA Cup hoodoo was about to strike again. Wrexham proved an easier task in the next round as they were despatched 5-0, and a solitary goal was enough to edge out Everton to secure a quarter-final trip to the south coast to face Bournemouth. A 2-1 win set up a semi-final against Birmingham City at Hillsborough, and the meeting with Villa was booked courtesy of a 2-0 win.

Yet on the big day it was not only the way the Wembley Final unfolded that was a disappointment to Albert Scanlon. A week before the match he had played in a 3-2 win against Cardiff City and scored two goals in a match where United had been reduced to ten men. He knew, though, that the performance offered only the most slender of chances of forcing his way into the team for Wembley and so it proved. When the squad departed for training at Blackpool he was not in the party.

He recalls: "I accepted it and travelled down on the Friday to the team hotel, although we didn't see the players. I didn't speak to them until after the match. Everybody knows what McParland did and the lads played well after we lost Ray Wood. Winning with ten fit men at the end of a long season was asking a lot and, to be, fair, I think the idea of a Double was built up more in the press than among the lads."

John Doherty was disappointed at missing out at Wembley, but like everyone else thought United would win as they were the best side in the country. He was watching the game with the official United party

Roger Byrne and Ray Wood cannot prevent giantkilling Bournemouth's centre-forward Brian Bedford scoring at Dean Court in March 1957, but there were no shocks as United won this FA Cup quarter-final game 2-1. Johnny Berry got both their goals. In earlier rounds, Bournemouth had knocked out Wolves and Spurs.

and has no doubt that the challenge on the goalkeeper by McParland was malicious. "McParland went and did Woody. There's no doubt about that. Certainly in today's football he wouldn't have stayed on the field. The team had deserved to win the Double and it was a great disappointment. Nobody argued with the referee because he had made his decision. That was an aspect of the game then. You accepted the ref had a job to do even if he got it wrong.

"There is no question in my mind that, but for the injury, United would have won the game. With a full side out for the 90 minutes they could have given Villa a two-goal lead and still won. At the evening dinner football wasn't really discussed. It was the end of the season and we were Champions again and there was nothing that could be done about what had happened earlier on the Wembley turf."

As an 11-year-old supporter Ian Boswell had collected enough tokens to ensure an FA Cup Final ticket. The token system was one of the great initiatives at Old Trafford, which ensured die hard supporters who had religiously followed the team through the season got to

Goalkeeper Ray Wood is carried off after a clash with Aston Villa's Peter McParland in the 1957 FA Cup Final.

see the Final. At other clubs it was a frequent complaint that when the big matches came around the tickets were siphoned off to those in the know rather than genuine fans. The token system ensured that was not the case with United.

Yet, as he recalls, Boswell was not at the match. "My parents decided I was too young to go which is understandable now, but at the time I was heartbroken. I had followed the team all season and had a Wembley ticket and I was going to miss out. Instead I watched the game with a group of friends crowded around a small black-and-white television set. If I was upset at missing out on Wembley it was all the worse when we lost."

For Roy Collins this was his first trip to Wembley, having accumulated enough tokens, and he confesses he was disappointed, not just with the result, but with the whole experience at the ground, from the food being expensive to the stadium not being as impressive as he imagined it. The match itself didn't help, of course. Like many of the fans, what hurt the most was that not only had United been deprived of the Double, but the manner in which the game was lost with the injury to the goalkeeper.

He said: "I was behind the goal and McParland just ran straight at Wood. He never seemed to slow up at all. In the crowd we couldn't believe it. It was just heartbreaking. Even by the standards of the 1950s it was a bad challenge. We couldn't believe it had happened. It was one of those awful moments. Usually the crowd is full of would-be refs and you get all sorts of views, but everyone was agreed about that."

With Wood off injured, Duncan Edwards moved to centre-half and for the first half United were able to keep the scoresheet clean. At one stage Wood returned and played on the wing to make up the numbers but nursing such a serious injury there was little he could do. Villa scored twice and, to heighten the sense of injustice felt by United's players and supporters, it was McParland who collected both of them. Taylor pulled a goal back and with United going all out for the equaliser Wood bravely returned between the posts, but it was not to be and the Double was gone.

Duncan Edwards and stand-in goalkeeper Jackie Blanchflower watch the ball go narrowly wide. Peter McParland, 'villain' of the afternoon, looks on.

The goalscorer at Wembley, Tommy Taylor had begun his career with Barnsley after being spotted playing for a local pub side. An early knee injury that required two operations was overcome and he was back playing for his home town club, scoring 26 goals in 44 appearances. It was not long before he was attracting interest from further afield and Busby paid £29,999 to bring him to Old Trafford. He scored twice on his debut, against Preston North End, and from then on the goals kept on coming. To the delight of the fans on the terraces Taylor proved a veritable goalscoring machine, netting 128 times in 189 appearances.

Ten weeks after signing for United he was on tour with England in South America and went on to win 19 England caps and scored 16 international goals, before his life was cut short at Munich. He was another player whose loss was a blow not only to United but to England as he would have certainly led the attack in the 1958 World Cup finals.

Ray Wood hailed from the North East and it will be little consolation that he found fame more for the foul on him in the Cup Final than his exploits between the posts for United that saw him win two Championship medals. He was signed as an 18-year-old from Darlington in 1949 and the following day made his debut against Newcastle United. However, competition for the goalkeeper's jersey at United was fierce and he was challenging first Jack Crompton and then Reg Allen, which often meant he was relegated to the sidelines. He survived the Munich crash, but had already lost his place in goal to another survivor, Harry Gregg. After ten seasons at the club he joined Huddersfield Town in 1958.

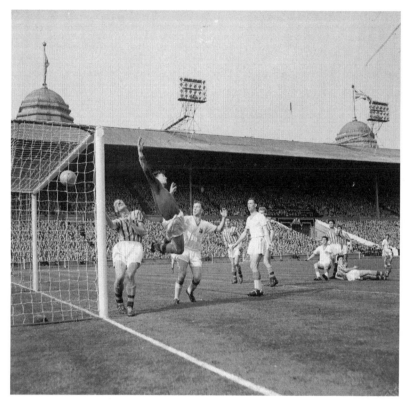

Aston Villa goalkeeper Nigel Sims fails to save United's only goal of the match, scored by Tommy Taylor, bending down on the right of the picture.

Although he was on a losing side, the young Duncan Edwards had already graced the stage that was Wembley, playing for England. Many thought his chance would come again with a young United side poised for further success. He was though to die of his injuries following the Munich disaster at the age of 21. He had already played in the United first team for five seasons and had achieved enough to have many still believing he was the greatest player to pull on the red shirt.

He won 18 caps and secured the record as the youngest player to play for England when he took the field against Scotland in April 1955 aged just 18 years and 183 days. A record that lasted for 33 years until Liverpool's Michael Owen took his international bow. The keenness with which Busby wanted to secure his talents was underlined by the fact he travelled to the West Midlands to get the youngster's signature on a contract just two hours after his 16th birthday. Jimmy Murphy had already visited the family home in Dudley to convince them their son's future lay at Old Trafford.

Bobby Charlton is reputed to have said of the powerful wing-half, with a hefty shot in either boot, that he was the only player to make him feel inferior and the best player he had lined up alongside for either United or England.

One honour the great Edwards was deprived of, though, was an FA Cup winners' medal. And the McParland incident still strikes a raw nerve with Charlton after all these years. "I saw him by chance at Tokyo airport a few years ago but I didn't speak to him. There is no point discussing the incident now. It is water under the bridge. These days what he did would be enormous news and would be in the papers for weeks. In the 1950s we just got on with things."

Forward into Europe

THERE are many qualities rightly attributed to Matt Busby and one that benefited, not just Manchester United but the whole of English football, was his belief in the importance of Europe and that the best teams in this country should test their mettle on a bigger stage.

England's supreme self-confidence in its own abilities and its rather disparaging view of football beyond its borders was comprehensively shattered by the arrival of the Hungarian side in 1953 that inflicted a 6-3 defeat at Wembley. Yet there was still a parochial air about the football establishment in this country.

The 1955-56 season saw the inauguration of a new European competition. The European Cup was open to the champions from various European Leagues and the first team from England to qualify was Chelsea. However, the Football League directed they should not enter.

The following year it was United's turn and Busby was not going to pass up the chance for his Red Devils to pit themselves against the best of Europe whatever the views of the powers that be. He persuaded the club's directors to support his view. And from now on Manchester United's horizons stretched beyond domestic competitions, and for Busby lifting the new European Cup would become his footballing Holy Grail.

Busby himself later said that, whether his defiance led to him being thought of as visionary, reactionary or even stubborn, he was determined to be a part of the new European competition and the challenges it represented. It was, he thought, only natural that the best in England should pit themselves against their counterparts in Europe and the game in this country could only benefit from such exposure.

Bobby Charlton is aware of how insular football in England was until Manchester United paved the way for clubs to take part in European football. As a player he was aware of the European sides by name but, in the days before television brought football from around the world into everyone's homes, no one was sure of the standard of football being played. Suddenly the European Cup made football fans sit up and take notice and added an interesting dimension to the domestic game.

He added: "Matt Busby was a prime mover in this country in widening the football horizons. He had great vision. It was not just the football, but he also saw the future with regard to the commercial side of the game and the opportunities European football could bring."

There could not have been a better start when United took their home bow in the competition against RSC Anderlecht on 26 September 1956. When they travelled to Brussels, United won 2-0 though it had been a close contest and the Belgians hit the post with a penalty, but goals by Dennis Viollet and Tommy Taylor gave United a valuable advantage for the return played at Maine Road rather than Old Trafford, which still did not have floodlights.

The Babes, though, were in no need of an advantage as they ran up a cricket score against Anderlecht, winning 10-0 with a display that later brought praise from Busby, who was delighted at seeing what he knew was a great side play close to the best of their abilities.

Bobby Charlton was in the Army doing National Service as the early rounds unfolded. He remembers travelling to Maine Road for the midweek game against Anderlecht. He had secured leave from the Army by taking his Company Sergeant Major with him from Shrewsbury where he was based. He was also at the game against Athletic Bilbao purely as a spectator.

Yet for many fans the scoreline perhaps merely reinforced their prejudices about European football. With hindsight there is talk of how all Manchester, or certainly the Red half of it, was excited at the prospect of European football. Others saw it differently.

Keen fan John Prestage was not at the match because he was working, and he confesses that at first the idea of European competition had not gripped him as it had some. "I think myself and a few others thought we were better than the European sides and the result against Anderlecht merely confirmed that. There was a feeling that we would win the European Cup now that we were the first English club to enter. I'd heard of Real Madrid, but never seen them so it was all new to me."

Only one player in the starting line-up in Brussels, as Manchester United began their European odyssey, would take the field 11 years later when the European Cup was won on a memorable night at Wembley. That man was Bill Foulkes. What a roller-coaster Europe would provide, with some of the highlights of his playing career, and also the worst with the disaster at Munich.

Yet while some United fans may have been sceptical about the European Cup, across the nation people were delighted to have a successful club competing against foreign opposition, given the travails of a national side that was still smarting from its defeats against Hungary. When Borussia Dortmund arrived at Maine Road 75,598 were packed into the ground.

With 27 minutes gone United had a 2-0 lead and when David Pegg benefited from a deflection for the third everything appeared to be going the home side's way, but this was not going to be the same cake-walk as the Anderlecht game. The Germans fought back and two goals for the visitors meant the return leg would not be a foregone conclusion.

A crowd of more than 44,000 in Dortmund included British Army national servicemen serving in Germany and they gave vocal support as the Reds fought to cling on to their advantage. A fine defensive display coupled with the luck needed on such occasions ensured the game finished goalless and United were in the next round.

John Doherty describes the performance of Ray Wood against Borussia Dortmund as 'the best game I ever saw him play'. In the freezing cold, Wood turned in a magnificent performance to keep a clean sheet.

Next up was Athletic Bilbao and this proved a tougher task. The opening leg was in Spain and United found themselves three goals down at half-time and facing an exit from the competition. After the break the Reds needed to quickly wrest the initiative from the Spanish side and this they did, with two goals within eight minutes courtesy of Tommy Taylor and Dennis Viollet.

It spurred Athletic Bilbao into action and they restored their three-goal lead before Billy Whelan scored a priceless effort – the pick of the goals in the heavy, muddy conditions. He went past three defenders before firing home and, while the task ahead was difficult, the goal at least threw United a lineline.

Rightly regarded as one of the best teams in Europe, Bilbao were confident that United would not be able to score three goals against them and as the game progressed at Maine Road before a 70,000 crowd, it seemed that Spanish confidence was not misplaced. The fates seemed to be conspiring against United. They had two goals ruled out for offside before Viollet scored just before the break. With six minutes remaining Taylor brought the teams level on aggregate and then the centre-forward was instrumental in setting up Johnny Berry for the winner.

Albert Scanlon recalls the Bilbao game as the most exciting European tie involving Manchester United. "We had to score three goals at Maine Road and the performance was a one-off. That was probably the best European Cup game I've seen. There was 70,000 packed in and many others who couldn't get a ticket. The touts were asking £25 for a 13s 6d ticket. That was how desperate people wanted to get in and how European football had caught the pubic imagination. I was disappointed not

Mark Jones and Bill Foulkes defend a cross during the European Cup quarter-final second leg game against Athletic Bilbao at Maine Road in February 1957.

to be playing in the competition. It was something new and fresh and we were the first English club taking part."

The semi-final saw the Babes pitched against another Spanish side, the formidable Real Madrid, whose line-up included Alfredo Di Stefano, a player Busby was to describe as the best he had ever seen. Before a crowd of 120,000 at the Bernabeu Stadium the first hour was deadlocked, but then the Spanish stepped up a gear and went into a two-goal lead before Taylor pulled one back. Crucially, though, the last word went to the home side with a late goal that meant United faced an uphill task in the second leg.

Charlton recalls: "They were exciting games. For the semi-final I travelled to Madrid and that was the first time it was brought home to me the quality of the best sides in Europe. I watched the game from up in the stands and they were the best. Di Stefano was outstanding. I marvelled at the quality and influence he brought to the game. David Pegg had a good game but they beat us 3-1."

Charlton remembers it was a measure of the professionalism of the Real Madrid side that by the time of the replay they had raided the transfer market for a player given the specific job of ensuring Pegg would not be such a dominant influence in the return match. Such additions to the squad would not be allowed now, but were within the rules in the 1950s.

With floodlights newly installed at Old Trafford the game could be played on home turf rather than across the city at Maine Road. Try as they might United found the Spanish were too good. They went 2-0 ahead and though the Babes earned a draw on the night, through goals from Charlton and Whelan, the meeting with the reigning champions of Europe had been a sobering experience and had shown players and supporters that there was still a gulf between United and

Real Madrid's Raymond Kopa scores his side's first goal in the European Cup semi-final second leg match at Old Trafford in April 1957. The scores was 2-2 on the night but United went down 5-3 on aggregate.

the best in Europe. Real went on to underline their class by retaining the European Cup by defeating Fiorentina of Italy in the Final.

Charlton himself was selected for the return, but remembers it was a daunting task. "United had come back from two goals down before, but not against a side like Real Madrid. They played on the break, which was new to us and, although the atmosphere was sensational, we found ourselves 2-0 down. We got to grips with them and got to the pace of the game but it was too late. We scored two goals and, if we had another ten minutes, we might have won but we ran out of time. We learned a lot playing such a quality side. They were exceptional. We were better prepared for how to approach the big European games after that."

Doherty, watching from the sidelines, was left in no doubt about the gulf between United and the Spanish giants. "Madrid were better than us. We had a cracking side, but they were better. They had magnificent players. Their side was packed with stars. It was like being up against a World XI side with players from all nations. Yet but for the Munich disaster the Busby Babes would have been the major challengers to Real Madrid. Apart from Madrid that Manchester United side would have been light years better than anyone else, especially in England."

Watching from the terraces Roy Collins agrees, saying: "I missed the start of the game because the swing bridge was open and there were a frustrating few minutes wasted watching people fishing before I could get in the ground. We had heard about the team and the magnificent stadium they had with the Bernabeu, but this was my first chance to see them in action. What a team they were. The best I've ever seen. You could see why Matt Busby was so keen to emulate them."

Retaining the League title meant that United did not have to wait long for another crack at European glory and a trip to Shamrock Rovers in the preliminary round offered the gentlest of obstacles to overcome as they travelled to Ireland and inflicted a 6-0 drubbing on the Irish champions. It was closer back at Old Trafford, with the Reds winning 3-2 to book a date with Dukla Prague in round one proper.

Prague were beaten 3-0 with Taylor and David Pegg being joined on the scoresheet by one of the lesser lights at Old Trafford. Colin Webster was more usually a reserve player but enjoyed his night on the centre stage in front of 60,000 and the goal was just reward for the inside-forward. A sound defensive display on their travels meant that despite losing 1-0 United were through.

As Busby started to ring the changes to his established starting line-up a number of players were given their chance in the first team including Albert Scanlon, who finally managed to dislodge David Pegg from the outside-left spot. He announced his return with a goal in a 4-0 defeat of Leicester City that marked the beginning of a seven-match unbeaten run in the League with some impressive results that included a 7-2 defeat of Bolton Wanderers in which Scanlon was again on the scoresheet.

Scanlon recalls: "Players like myself, Harry Gregg, Bobby Charlton and Kenny Morgans were given our chance and we had an impressive run of results. Busby was never afraid to make changes and the new players performed well. It was the new players coming through who were given their chance in Europe when we played the next round."

Red Star Belgrade were the next opponents and, although the Yugoslavs opened the scoring when the teams met at Old Trafford, goals by Eddie Colman and Charlton gave the Reds the slenderest of leads to take to Belgrade. It proved enough as a United side that had hit a rich seam of form took a three-goal lead with two for Charlton and with Viollet also netting. Shortly after the restart Belgrade pulled one back and then won a penalty to leave everything to play for.

Three minutes from time goalkeeper Harry Gregg was penalised for holding the ball outside his area and the free-kick was hammered past him. It was 3-3 but United held on for a semi-final place.

Scanlon recalls: "We should have been four up but the referee blew up for offside and I had centred the ball from a corner. The ref went absolutely barmy after that. Their players were falling down and he was giving them everything. We did well to hold on for a draw given the decisions of the referee. The crowd also got hostile and at one point they were throwing ice and bottles."

Despite the problems for the players the result was a good one, but the match was to become memorable for all the wrong reasons. The return flight to Manchester would end in disaster and mark one of the saddest days in the annals of soccer history. As we shall see, many of the team built by Busby and dubbed his Babes would not go any further than Munich on the return journey. The air crash destroyed a team but helped establish the name and reputation of Manchester United far beyond the boundaries of the city.

When the semi-final was played against AC Milan it was a vastly different side that took the field although there was still confidence among some of the supporters, however misplaced it might have been. Indeed, a 2-1 win at Old Trafford raised the spectre of United achieving the impossible. On first reading the goalscorers seemed to have a familiar air about them. Taylor and Viollet got the goals, but this was not Tommy, the England centre-forward whose life had been tragically lost at Munich. In the rebuilding programme that hastily followed the crash the first player signed was the veteran Ernie Taylor from Blackpool.

Manchester United embark on a trip aboard a Royal Mail plane prior to their European Cup preliminary round match away to Shamrock Rovers which they won 6-0 in September 1957: Left to right: Bill Foulkes, Ray Wood, Dennis Viollet, Jackie Blanchflower, Peter Jones, Alex Dawson, Roger Byrne, Tommy Taylor, Duncan Edwards, Eddie Colman, David Pegg, Mark Jones.

The dream of Europe ended on the return with AC Milan running out comfortable 4-0 winners. It would be five years before United again set out to compete on the Continent and another decade before Matt Busby would finally realise his dream and lift the European Cup. In the aftermath of the Munich disaster that all seemed a long way off.

The Munich Disaster

THE performance against Red Star Belgrade was to be overshadowed by events that happened as the Busby Babes made their journey home. The side that Matt Busby had so carefully and painstakingly put together would be decimated in minutes. A nation would be thrown into a state of shock. And Manchester United as a club would never be the same again.

What the side could have achieved, but for the Munich air disaster on 6 February 1958, will never be known. Certainly some of the greatest players of their generation were lost,

Highbury, February 1958, and United's last League game before the Munich disaster. Top: Harry Gregg covers the ball as Arsenal's Jimmy Bloomfield takes a tumble. Duncan Edward has his arms outstretched while Roger Byrne, Bill Foulkes and Mark Jones are the other United defenders. Bottom: In front of the Arsenal goal with Dennis Viollet and Tommy Taylor airborne.

either killed or having suffered injuries that effectively ended their careers. In the sporting world where hyperbole is commonplace this was truly a tragedy of epic proportions.

The facts of the disaster are well documented. The twin-engined Elizabethan plane the team were travelling in stopped at Munich to refuel. The weather was worsening and snow was beginning to fall. It took barely 20 minutes to refuel the plane and the United party hoped to be back in Manchester for teatime.

The first attempt at a take-off was abandoned after the pilot thought the engines had an uneven note. A second attempt was also aborted. The plane returned to the airport terminus and the players disembarked while the problem was investigated. While some of the players bought presents and cigarettes, others were becoming concerned at the situation. Many hoped the journey might be completed overland via the Hook of Holland.

Albert Scanlon recalls that there was a pressure to be back because United had defied the authorities in playing in the competition and they would not tolerate any postponement of their next game or United fielding a weakened side. He believes it was this that ensured the United party boarded the plane despite misgivings among the players.

United board their plane at Ringway Airport in Manchester to fly to Belgrade to play in the European Cup.

He remembers that eventful night more than 40 years on. "We had got off for a coffee while the plane refuelled and then we all got back on board, but it didn't go and we turned back. We tried the second time and that didn't happen. When we got off for the third time I was joking that we should catch the train home. Looking back on it now we would have got home safely if we had.

"A lot of the players were unhappy about getting back on the plane, but once it was announced we were going there was really no choice. It would have taken a very brave man to say he wasn't getting on the plane. No one was going to do it. A lot of us were youngsters and none of us would have argued with the decision. It would have needed to be a senior player."

Sure enough, when the call came to reboard the aircraft they all filed out, with any reluctance on the part of individuals kept to them-

Matt Busby addresses his team in their Belgrade hotel.

selves. There was, though, to be another twist. Alf Clarke, a journalist with the *Manchester Evening Chronicle*, was left behind because he was on the phone filing copy to his paper. The plane was delayed for him. It was a decision that would cost him his life.

As they sat waiting for take-off some of the players who

were not good fliers were starting to get nervous, including captain Roger Byrne and Johnny Berry. The plane began its third attempt to take off. The aircraft careered off the runway and hit a house, which tore off a wing and part of the tail. The cockpit hit a tree and the fuselage collided with a

wooden hut, causing the truck inside to go up in flames.

Goalkeeper Harry Gregg fought free of the wreckage and was urged to make his escape by one of the pilots. At that moment he heard a baby crying and dashed back into the wreckage to save both the child and its mother. He kept returning to help others still trapped, pulling both Bobby Charlton and Dennis Viollet clear. He also helped a badly injured Matt Busby and Jackie Blanchflower.

Scanlon's memory of the accident is brief. "I remember taking off and everything after that is just a blank. I was unconscious for a long while. It was ten days later before I came round. It was only years later that I learned we had hit a tree."

Emergency services arrived at the scene and took the dead and injured to Munich's Rechts Der Isar Hospital. Busby had suffered punctured lungs and broken legs and, twice, the last rites were administered as he lay in an oxygen tent. His battling qualities saw him through and, although it was a long fight, he was eventually able to return to Manchester after 71 days.

Years later he would recall that one of the most heartrending moments was listening to the injured Johnny Berry berate his best friend Tommy Taylor for not visiting him in hospital. It wasn't what best mates did, Berry would complain to the manager. Nobody had yet told Berry that his friend was dead. Berry himself had suffered injuries which ended a career that had spanned seven seasons since he joined United from Birmingham City for £15,000 in 1951 and had seen him win three Championship medals.

The last time... United line-up before the European Cup quarter-final second leg game against Red Star Belgrade in February 1958. Left to right are Duncan Edwards, Eddie Colman, Mark Jones, Ken Morgans, Bobby Charlton, Dennis Viollet, Tommy Taylor, Billy Foulkes, Harry Gregg, Albert Scanlon and Roger Byrne.

Red Star goalkeeper Vladimir Beara punches clear from Viollet and Taylor in Belgrade.

The wreckage of the BOAC Elizabethan charter flight which was carrying the Manchester United team back from Belgrade. After a refuelling stop at Munich, the plane crashed as it tried to take off on the snowy runway, killing 23 people, including eight players.

Back home Manchester was in a state of shock. Like the assassination of President Kennedy, it was one of those moments where everyone remembers where they were when they heard the news of the fate that had befallen the Manchester United team. Fan Ian Boswell had returned home from his paper round. He says: "It was just so hard to grasp what had happened. We waited for the news of the players. My favourite player was Roger Byrne and it came through that he had died."

David Hollingworth had just started work and was told of the disaster as he made his way home. He says simply: "I thought 'this is the end of football. There is no way United can come back after this.'"

Kevin Smith was ten, and the youngest of three brothers who were all called into the house and sat down on the settee to be told the news. "It was as though there had been a death in the family. I can remember it as though it was yesterday."

The great Manchester United team which was destroyed at Munich. Back row (left to right): Eddie Colman, Bill Foulkes, Ray Wood, Roger Byrne, Mark Jones and Duncan Edwards. Front: Dennis Viollet, Johnny Berry, Tommy Taylor, Bill Whelan, David Pegg.

Roy Collins was at work when rumours started circulating that there had been an accident involving footballers. Details were sketchy and in a big workshop things tended to get exaggerated so he waited until he got home and heard the full extent of the tragedy unfold on the radio. "The colour just drained from my face when I heard the news. It was an emotional time for everybody. I couldn't think of anything more terrible. I just sat listening to the radio as the latest reports on individual players were announced."

Bill Makin remembers the line of buses filing past Old Trafford as they brought workers home from Trafford Park had a funereal air. It was, he recalls, as though they were a funeral cortege flowing past the ground where many of the players now dead or injured had performed so magnificently. "I don't think there was a dry eye in any of those buses and there must have been thousands on board. Most of us thought this was the end of football as we had known it."

The nation waited and prayed as Duncan Edwards fought for his life. Strong as he was, he lost his fight after 15 days. He had suffered horrific injuries that included a shattered right thigh, broken ribs, a collapsed lung, a broken pelvis and liver damage, yet at one stage was still able to joke with Jimmy Murphy that he would be back for the next game. Tragically, it was not to be. A man who could lay claim to being one of England's greatest footballers was dead at the age of 21, with only a fraction of his potential fulfilled.

Twenty-one died in the wreckage or soon after. Two others, including Edwards, would swell the number. Eight United players were among the victims: Roger Byrne, Tommy Taylor, Duncan Edwards, Eddie Colman, Mark Jones, Bill Whelan, Geoff Bent and David Pegg. Two other players, Johnny Berry and Jackie Blanchflower, both survived but their injuries ensured their football careers were over. United coach Bert Whalley and trainer Tom Curry were also killed along with secretary Walter Crickmer.

Eight journalists also perished including Clarke, who had caused the delay. Their number also included Frank Swift, the former Manchester City and England goalkeeper who was working for the *News of the World*.

It was only fate that decreed Ian Greaves was not on the plane. As Manchester United had prepared to fly out for their tragic European Cup tie he had been playing for the Reserves. "I had been told to bring my kit and travelling bag with me because I was

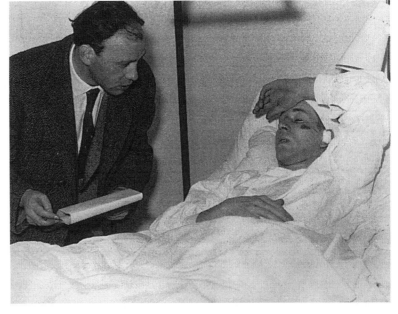

Bobby Charlton, in his hospital bed, manages a few words with a journalist.

expecting to go as a replacement," he recalls. "In the bath after the match the assistant trainer Jimmy Murphy came in and told me I wasn't going. They were taking my best mate Geoff Bent as cover for Roger Byrne who was carrying an injury. Geoff never came back. I now celebrate two birthdays every year. One is on the day of the crash on 6 February because, but for the Grace of God, it would have been me there. I give a thought to the lads each year."

By an unhappy coincidence the day of the disaster was also the day that former Busby Babe John Doherty was undergoing the knee operation that was to end his football career after just a dozen games for First Division side Leicester City. "I think God had decided that whether I stayed at Old Trafford or left I wasn't going to play football after 6 February. In hospital I was not aware of what had happened until a boy came round with the papers and there was a special edition, which he brought for me because he thought he was doing a favour, but it was the last thing I needed at that time, as I recovered from the operation."

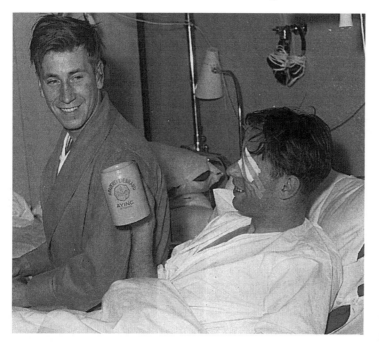

In better spirits, Bobby Charlton chats with goalkeeper Ray Wood in the Rechts der Isar Hospital.

England and Bolton Wanderers centre-forward Nat Lofthouse remembers a League game against Manchester United a few weeks before the disaster in the middle of January. Bolton were on the wrong end of a 7-2 hiding. While there might have been no love lost between the fans the players of the two clubs always got on well. In the United dressing-room were bottled beers and a bottle opener and Lofthouse went in for a chat and a drink. He joked with the United players that they must have been worried as Bolton had enjoyed a late rally. Sixteen days later, many of those players with whom he had shared a drink were dead.

Another player for England and Bolton Wanderers, the full-back Tommy Banks, believes the ramifications of the disaster affected him personally and English football in ways beyond the sheer horror of a tragedy that robbed the world of fine footballers. He is honest enough to admit that he would probably have never worn the England shirt but for the crash. The England full-back was Manchester United's Roger Byrne. "I know I was lucky to get in the England team. I think I would have been in the party for the World Cup, but as the reserve full-back," says Banks.

The Bolton player is on record that, without the disaster, England would have won the World Cup in Sweden in 1958. "I have always said we would have won the World Cup. I am convinced of it. That year we held Brazil to a goalless draw with a scratch team. With the Manchester United players who were lost the World Cup would have been ours eight years earlier than it was, and Manchester United would have been European champions in 1958. That's how much English football was set back."

Jimmy Murphy was handed the task of putting together a side to meet Sheffield Wednesday in the fifth round of the FA Cup. Two players were bought to bolster the side, with Ernie Taylor joining

Goalkeeper Harry Gregg, assistant manager Jimmy Murphy and defender Bill Foulkes look from the window of the train as they depart from Munich to travel by land back to England.

from Blackpool for £8,000 and Stan Crowther leaving Aston Villa for £24,000. Both were given special permission to play for United in the Cup, despite having already played for their old teams.

As well as the new signings a number of youngsters from the Reserves were drafted into the team. There was a huge roar as the players emerged followed by a minute's silence for the victims of Munich dutifully observed by the close to 60,000 crowd. The game was a roller coaster of emotions.

John Prestage recalls: "A huge crowd had made its way to the ground, but many of us weren't sure if there would be a game and whether United could get a team together.

It was an incredible atmosphere full of emotion. The programme contained just blanks where the names of the United players should have been. Suddenly there was a huge roar as the first name was announced. It was Harry Gregg, one of the Munich survivors. Then another great cheer as the second name was another who had survived the crash, Bill Foulkes.

"After the minute's silence the match started and it wasn't one that anybody could have really expected us to win, but Sheffield weren't playing a makeshift team they were up against a whole crowd of thousands willing the side on. It was a cauldron. Certainly it was the most emotional match that I've attended. It was a hell of an experience that game."

He remembers one of the players for Sheffield was Albert Quixall who would soon be joining United. He was one of the stars of his day but he could do nothing to save the tie for the visitors. Prestage said: "When the first goal went in there was another huge roar. I'm convinced it was the supporters who carried the team through that first game. In fairness, Sheffield Wednesday must have found it difficult at that time and it was said afterwards they didn't play as well as they could have done given the circumstances of the match.

Bobby Charlton, physiotherapist Ted Dalton and Jimmy Murphy watch United in action against Sheffield Wednesday in February 1958, the first game after Munich.

United opened the scoring through Shay Brennan, whose corner found its way into the net thanks to a slip by the Sheffield goalkeeper, and the Irishman scored the second when he seized on a shot that rebounded off the helpless goalkeeper. Mark Pearson, one of the reserve players drafted into the side, pulled the ball back for Alex Dawson to score and United's remarkable journey to Wembley was under way.

The match programme contained the famous rallying cry: "United Will Go On," delivered by chairman Harold Hardman. On the front of the *United Review* he wrote that the Munich crash was a tragedy that would sadden everyone for years to come and wherever football was played, United would be mourned.

And he added: "Although we mourn our dead and grieve for our wounded, we believe that great days are not done for us. The sympathy and encouragement of the football world and particularly of our supporters will justify and inspire us. The road back may be long and hard, but with the memory of those who died at Munich, of their stirring achievements and wonderful sportsmanship ever with us, Manchester United will rise again."

The Post-Munich Cup Final

THE 1958 FA Cup Final was the 30th played at Wembley and one of the most emotive and controversial, although it is fair to say, not the most artistic. It pitted Bolton, who had not bought a player in eight years, against Manchester United, struggling to create a new generation of Busby Babes after the horrors of the Munich air disaster.

The old clash in styles was still there. Bolton were deemed workmanlike. There were no claims to glamour and their only star was Nat Lofthouse, though there were question marks over how well he had recovered from the shoulder injury that kept him out of the semi-final. They were considered a strong defensive side, but also capable of producing brilliant, attacking moves at times.

New-look Manchester United in March 1958. Back row (left to right): Bobby Harrop, Ian Greaves, Freddie Goodwin, Harry Gregg, Stan Crowther, Ronnie Cope, Shay Brennan. Front: Jack Crompton (trainer), Alex Dawson, Stan Pearson, Bill Foulkes, Ernie Taylor, Colin Webster, Bill Inglis (assistant trainer).

Meanwhile, as they had in the years before and would continue to do so until this day, United were the team that trawled the country looking to find players, and for them money was no object. There was also a sense that many of the young players being given their chance were talented and would have made the first teams at other clubs probably far sooner. It is a situation echoed in the squad system at Old Trafford today.

The fervour with which the nation willed the success of United was captured in a hyperbole-strewn front page editorial in the *Manchester Evening News* on the eve of the Final that said: "Manchester United's Red Devils have won through to Wembley again... it takes your breath away, it defies reason, it thrills, and it makes you both proud and humble. This is the most wondrous thing in the history of football, an epic story fired by death and the will to live. The Red Devils have not merely survived, they have added yet another chapter of success and the club is gloriously alive again."

Matt Busby returns home to Manchester in April 1958, discharged from the Rechts der Isar Hospital.

Such outpourings of support left the Bolton players in no doubt that, their 15,000 supporters in the ground aside, the Wembley crowd and the nation was urging a United win and a fairytale finish for them in such a heartbreaking season. Memories of Stanley Matthews and the 1953 Final came flooding back when the Bolton team had the role of bit part players in a dramatic 4-3 last gasp win for Blackpool that saw the great Matthews finally win the medal he dreamed of.

There was another old face from the Blackpool Final who was back to face them. Ernie Taylor, who had been a key figure in Bolton's late demise, with his accurate passing finally unleashing Matthews and setting up the famous win, would now be providing the same service for Dennis Viollet and Bobby Charlton. The England international was now 32.

Manchester United had history on their side, though in their case it had been compromised by the Munich air crash. On all four previous occasions when the defeated Finalists had gone back to Wembley on the first attempt they had gone home with the trophy. Experience of the Wembley atmosphere was seen as giving the team the edge, but in United's case six of the previous year's team had been killed and three were seriously injured.

Ian Greaves recalls it was a new team in many ways, with some players recently acquired and others who hadn't really played first-team football. He had played 20 first-team games and that marked him down as almost a veteran. However, as the team battled through the FA Cup rounds, a spirit had begun to develop and by the Final a real camaraderie had been forged.

"Good players can get you to the top but so can team spirit and we started to feel we could play a bit. Perhaps we didn't know what we were doing properly, but we had gelled into an outfit that was already proving hard to beat, though we were certainly not the most talented team United have had," he said.

Bolton full-back Tommy Banks, though, remembers there was a confidence in their side and everybody was relaxed. While they were up against the will of the nation, on the field the Manchester United side were now tragically a shadow of the team that beat them 7-2 in a League game only months before. Banks recalls: "I was never as confident of winning a game as I was then. If I had been a betting man I would have had money on us. Everybody was against us as they were in 1953, but on the field there are still only 11 players facing you. To be honest I think we would have had a good game even if it was their full team."

Greaves remembers it was three days before the events of the day fully sank in. He can recall walking out with the teams and the shivers were running down his spine. "There is something wonderful about Wembley. Even now in places like Italy and Germany the players there still think it is the place. It's always held that thrill. As I walked out I thought we could do it. We had got this far and we had the mental determination to go on."

John Prestage had been to every game in the run up to the Final except the semi-final against Fulham. "There was a feeling that we could win the Cup though it was based more on blind faith than any realistic assessment of our chances. We had a scratch team and yet we believed we could do the seemingly impossible and lift the Cup. Some were even convinced the European Cup could be won as well. It was an unbelievable time as people were swept along with the idea."

When United beat West Bromwich Albion, after a replay, to secure

Matt Busby takes a
back seat at Wembley
for the 1958 FA Cup
Final. His assistant,
Jimmy Murphy, is on
the bench.

Manchester United captain Bill Foulkes (partly hidden) introduces the Duke of Edinburgh to Bobby Charlton before the 1958 FA Cup Final.

a semi-final place the idea that this was the Reds' year was reinforced. West Brom had been held to a 2-2 draw at The Hawthorns and then United edged it by a solitary goal at Old Trafford. Prestage has memories of one of the earlier ties when in the third round, United travelled to Workington. The match pre-dated Munich but sticks in his mind as the worst ground he visited in all his years watching the Reds.

He recalls: "What had made matters worse was the train was overcrowded and then was delayed at Grange-over-Sands for what seemed like hours. I'd never heard of the place before but there was a nice beach and people were joking we should forget the game and spend a few hours on the sand. When we arrived at the ground it was a dump. There was nothing there except a tin shed for a stand. We won 3-1 and everyone couldn't wait to get back home. Following United you didn't get to see grounds like that too often."

The Reds needed a replay to get past Fulham. They drew 2-2 at Villa Park and then travelled to Arsenal's Highbury Stadium when, in an impressive display, they came through 5-3. With the team playing beyond anybody's wildest expectations the Cup dream was still on.

Prestage had sent off his tokens and his 2s 6d (12½p) Cup Final ticket duly arrived by registered post. With friends, who also worked on the railways, he travelled to Wembley and remembers it was a glorious day. Before the match they repaired to a pub and sat in the sunshine enjoying a pint before the match. Having come so far they were all confident of victory although any neutral would have made Bolton favourites.

He recalls: "There was friendly banter with the Bolton fans. We felt that having come so far we were fated to win. If we had beaten other teams to get here then why not Wanderers as well."

The game itself was a dour affair decided by two Lofthouse goals. The second of which was the infamous barge on United goalkeeper Harry Gregg that will forever be shrouded in controversy. Nowadays the centre-forward would have been lucky to escape with a yellow rather than a red card. Then the goal stood.

But Lofthouse himself now admits: "It was a very emotive game and the question I am always asked after Gregg was bundled into the net is was it a foul or not? Yes it was. I have always been glad that we won by two goals. I see Harry quite often and he doesn't bother about it because he is a hell of a guy. When you consider this was a guy who went back into the aircraft to try and rescue some of his teammates that is a measure of the man."

Gregg had only recently got into the United side, replacing Ray Wood after signing from Doncaster Rovers in December 1957, and he was to put the disappointment of Wembley behind him later that year when he turned in some sterling efforts for Northern Ireland in the 1958 World Cup finals in Sweden. Gregg's career started in Irish League football before Doncaster Rovers signed him in 1951. He cost United £23,500, establishing a new British transfer record for a goalkeeper to bring him to Old Trafford where he was to remain for nine seasons, amassing nearly 250 first-team appearances before signing for Stoke City in 1966.

Tommy Banks jokes that when he sees Gregg, he always tells him: "Thou were swanking knocking it up saying `it's mine.' People,

Nat Lofthouse, far left of picture, scores Bolton's first goal in the 1958 Cup Final. Harry Gregg is well beaten and Stan Crowther cannot get back to cover.

though, talk about that goal, but to be honest they never looked like scoring apart from a Bobby Charlton shot that hit the post. It was unfortunate, and I'm not saying they wouldn't have won if it had been disallowed. You can't say that. But on the day we deserved it and I think we always had a bit of a downer on United. We always played well against them."

On the terraces Prestage and the United fans he was with saw things very differently. For them this was 1957 and the McParland charge on Ray Wood revisited. "But for Lofthouse scoring with a foul on the goalkeeper I'm still convinced we could have won the game. That was the view of everybody around me at the time and afterwards. We felt we had been robbed. The goal seemed to knock the stuffing out of the players."

Lofthouse's opener came in the third minute when he met a long ball from Edwards. United were given little chance to shine and their attacking efforts were minimal. The best chance fell to Charlton in the 54th minute; his fierce shot hit a post and rebounded into Hopkinson's grateful hands. Three minutes later a Stevens shot was pushed into the air by Gregg, Lofthouse powered in, goalkeeper and ball were in the net – and the game was effectively over.

Harry Gregg lies flattened in the United goalmouth after Nat Lofthouse's challenge bundled both ball and goalkeeper into the net.

Greaves thought he had played well enough and afterwards, because United had the sympathy vote, there was no real criticism of the players. He remembers going up for his medal and forgetting the last instruction to take his chewing gum out so he went to the Royal Box chewing away. He is full of praise for the Bolton side and adds that nothing can be taken away from their performance.

Such was the way the events of the Munich disaster hung over the game that Bolton's Roy Hartle reveals that he and Banks nearly didn't bother with the traditional lap of honour for the winners to parade the trophy. "We had been up to get our medals from the Royal Box and we walked back down and stood around and waited for someone to tell us to go on the lap of honour. I looked at Tommy Banks and he asked me what I thought and I said I didn't know. We were both going to walk off into the dressing-room when Bert Sproston, the trainer, came over and told us `you must do the lap of honour. It will be the biggest thing in your career and you will remember it all your life.' He was right as it turned out, but at the time we just couldn't see what all the fuss was about. After Munich the match was a bit meaningless I suppose."

Bolton goalkeeper Eddie Hopkinson saves from an Ernie Taylor header as Dennis Viollet races in.

Such was the disappointment for Prestage and his friends that they didn't bother going for a drink after the game or seeing any of the London sights. "We made our way to the train station, found our train in a sidings and just sat there for a few hours waiting to leave for home. Nobody hardly spoke everyone was feeling that down. It's a shame really because it was such a beautiful day we should have at least tried to do something."

Bobby Charlton takes a philosophical view of the Final. "Everybody was pleased that we had got there after the terrible accident. Going to the Cup Final seemed to be the sign that the club had recovered. Although we lost to Bolton I didn't think that it mattered so much. The mere fact that we were there, and had come back from the terrible thing that had happened, and there was a future, was enough. At one stage there had been a fear that we might get relegated and go under."

The Rebuilding Begins

WHEN he returned to his duties Matt Busby predicted it would be five years before Manchester United would be back winning trophies. He was aware of the enormity of the task ahead of him as he began the rebuilding that would restore United to greatness and produce a team to rival the Busby Babes so cruelly lost to the footballing world.

Bobby Charlton remembers that there was a rush to buy players even though everyone knew it was a short-term measure until Busby returned from his injuries and began the task of recreating a new Manchester United, steeped in his own philosophy of how the game should be played.

"He said it would take five years to bring the club to anything like it was before," recalls Charlton. "And it was almost five years to the day he made the prediction that we beat Leicester City in the Cup Final and then started looking again to be the first English team to lift the European Cup. Manchester United is a big club and there was a responsibility. The public expected it. That is part and parcel of United. The club is expected to be the best and play exciting football."

In the immediate aftermath of the tragedy the task was to ensure Manchester United had a team that could at least compete and recruits were quickly brought on board. The running of the team fell to assistant manager Jimmy Murphy, who had not been on the fateful trip to Belgrade because of international duties with Wales.

Charlton had been a player just breaking into the first team at the time of Munich, but now he would take on the responsibility as one of the senior players to help to first ensure United's survival and then to take the club forward to the pre-eminence it had enjoyed before the tragedy. The task could not have fallen on a more suitable pair of shoulders. He is reported to have said that, even after all that had happened at Munich and its aftermath, he never considered giving up football and, rather, sought solace in the game as he came to terms with the disaster.

As a player he grew to epitomise all that was best in a professional footballer. He was a supreme exponent of the game on the field with a versatility that meant he was effective as winger, inside-forward or centre-forward. He was also a role model for how to behave away from the ground. As the attractions of the 1960s saw numerous scandals involve the leading players of the day Charlton's behaviour was always impeccable.

Although in character they were widely different, George Best would later praise the skills of Charlton. His accurate passes, his powerful shooting and the aura he carried with him, of not just being a great footballer but also a gentleman known for his sportsmanship. He was one of the world's great footballers, but as he himself mentioned earlier in this book he had to wait longer than most at Old Trafford to get his first-team chance.

He was a nephew of the Newcastle United centre-forward Jackie Milburn, but though hailing from County Durham he became a fan of Manchester United having been seduced by the attacking talents of the great 1940s side. It is said he never missed a game when the Reds were playing in the North-East.

United goalkeeper Harry Gregg collects a high ball as Preston's Alec Farrall waits for a slip. United lost this game 4-0 at Deepdale in September 1959.

As a centre-forward at United he found himself in the shadow of Tommy Taylor and it was as an inside-right, in place of Billy Whelan that he had established himself just before the horror of Munich. As an England international in the 1960s he established what was then a record of 106 full caps and scored a record 49 goals. His greatest international moment was collecting a World Cup winners' medal as part of the 1966 side. The highlight with United was lifting the European Cup in 1968. In all he played more than 750 games and scored nearly 250 goals for the Reds.

Off the field he was voted Footballer of the Year and European Footballer of the Year in 1966. In 1994 he was the first footballer to be knighted since Stanley Matthews 30 years before. After 17 seasons at United since making his first-team debut, he joined Preston North End as manager, but life in the managerial role never worked out and he moved into business. He is also a director of Manchester United and was an ambassador for England's World Cup bid.

The Busby Babes had been well placed for title success when the disaster struck. The last match on home soil before the team set off for Belgrade and its date with destiny was a thriller. Arsenal were the opponents and more than 63,000 packed Highbury to watch two of the finest teams in the land go through their paces.

By half-time United were three goals to the good and seemingly cantering to an impressive win but there was to be plenty more action in the game. With 15 minutes of the second half gone Arsenal scored three goals in a devastating three-minute spell and suddenly there was a memorable contest in store.

The Reds fought back and a Dennis Viollet header restored the lead, which was increased with a Tommy Taylor shot from an acute angle. A late goal for Arsenal ensured the contest went to the wire but it was the visitors who held on to keep their title ambitions on track. Five days later events elsewhere would shatter such ambitions.

While they enjoyed a successful Cup run buoyed by their fans and the sympathy of a nation, the rest of the League programme turned into a hard slog. After their success at Highbury, United won only once more in their remaining 14 fixtures. The run included two 4-0 reverses at home, to West Bromwich Albion and Wolves. The solitary win was a 2-1 victory at Sunderland.

With Busby back the rebuilding task could begin and one of the first players recruited was Albert Quixall. He arrived for a British record fee of £45,000 from Sheffield Wednesday in September 1958. He was one of the stars of his era and fans remember him as having something of a playboy reputation with his youthful looks. He won five England caps and stayed at the club until 1964 when he moved to Oldham Athletic, having played nearly 200 games for United in his six seasons at the club.

The 1958-59 season seemed to defy all logic as the team turned in some superb displays to finish runners-up. Charlton scored a hat-trick in an opening 5-2 win at home to Chelsea and then bagged a brace in a 3-0 victory over Nottingham Forest. On 6 September, Blackburn Rovers were beaten 6-1 before the team's form hit something of a slump. There were just two wins in 13 games until a 2-1 home win against Luton Town towards the end of November sparked a remarkable run of form with a 12-match spell that saw 11 wins and a draw. The sequence was only ended by a 3-2 reverse against Arsenal at Highbury.

Albert Scanlon had made a recovery from his head and leg injuries suffered in the disaster and was now back on the left wing. Looking back he believes the Munich tragedy not only ruined the team that was in place, but because they were brought into the first team too quickly a lot of the youngsters waiting in the wings also had their careers damaged. "They were brought in before they were ready and many struggled. It was also difficult for the players that were bought like Ernie Taylor and Stan Crowther because they were joining many players who had been together since they were schoolboys."

Although Scanlon was back and was to be an ever-present for the League campaign and a valuable asset as United sought to rebuild he pondered the effects of the tragedy he had survived. "It's hard to know the effects of a tragedy like Munich on your career. I thought I was getting better and played the friendlies and pre-season games, but it's only when the season starts proper that you know if you are back. I played in every game and we finished runners-up, which given what had happened the season before was an impressive performance.

"It was not hard to concentrate on the football. The hard part was meeting the relatives of the players who had been lost. I didn't want to talk about what happened and there was always this feeling of 'why me?'. Why had I survived and others hadn't? I also didn't want to talk about their lad. I often used to wonder what they were thinking. Whether the thought was going through their minds 'why are you here and not my lad'. In the club itself and in the dressing-room Munich was never discussed. It must have been five or six years before I even mentioned it. I still think about the lads; what they would have gone on and done. Time stopped still for them and gave me a fresh start."

Charlton's partner up front, and with whom he shared 50 goals in the season, was Dennis Viollet. Manchester-born, he had joined United as a 16-year-old and was with the club for 13 years, playing in nearly 300 games. He was capped twice for England and his goalscoring prowess was underlined when he established a United goalscoring record of 32 League goals in the 1959-60 season. He was sold to Stoke City for £25,000 in 1962.

Viollet was aware of the burden on his young shoulders following Munich, that he had become a symbol of the new United and a favourite with the fans. He admitted that for someone as shy as him, all the fuss occasionally was too much. Particularly when there was a clamour for him to be included in the England team. Viollet died at his home in the USA in March 2002, aged 65, from a brain tumour.

An early, ignominious exit from the Cup, going down 3-0 to Norwich City of the Third Division, meant that United could concentrate on the League. In February, United joined the League leaders Wolverhampton Wanderers at the top of the table after defeating the Midlands club 2-1 at Old Trafford. The Reds had a good run-in to the end of the season losing only two of their last 11 games, but it was not good enough and they finished six points behind Wolves.

In the FA Cup tie against Norwich, Scanlon was aware of the pressure on United to return to Wembley for a third successive season and avenge the previous two Cup Final defeats. Particularly given the poignancy of the previous year when the post-Munich side had battled so hard to reach the Final, only to lose to Bolton Wanderers. Yet he can't recall anyone mentioning the previous year's defeat in the dressing-room before the game.

He says simply: "They took their chances and we didn't. It was icy and the players struggled to stand up and they adapted better. I can't take anything away from Norwich and to their credit they got to the semi-final that year. It was a day for belting the ball up the field and everybody running after it and that's what they did. We were obviously disappointed, but that's Cup football."

The next four seasons were not as kind to United as the rebuilding process slowly took shape, and Busby suffered the worst run in League form since he took charge of the club in 1946. United supporters were not used to seeing their team down among the League's also-rans. Their record of finishes reads 7th, 7th, 15th and 19th, although the shock of near-relegation in the 1962-63 season would be tempered by a successful FA Cup run.

Yet Kevin Smith remembers things differently. He was only ten at the time of the Munich disaster so the team he grew up with and supported was the one that was rebuilt after the tragedy. He remembers: "We always seemed to be improving. Many of the fans talked of the Busby Babes side, but for me my memories are of the new side that was taking shape. There seemed to be so many players arriving as Busby looked to create a new side. As far as I was concerned as soon as they signed for United they were stars."

The player to make the biggest impression on him in the early 1960s was Denis Law. He recalls: "As a kid I was taken to Blackpool and Law was playing. After the match all the youngsters got to the tunnel, because there was not the security there is today, to see the players. We met them all and then waited for them to go to the coach.

The only player who wasn't travelling on the coach was Law and he had a big white Jag. We were all impressed. He was the first super-star."

In 1959-60 season Viollet and Charlton again shared 50 goals and the former averaged nearly a goal a game for his 32, but any hopes that this campaign would emulate the previous one, and continue to confound those who couldn't believe United could bounce back from the disaster so quickly, were to be dashed. The long unbeaten runs that had characterised the previous year were missing and the team's form was patchy.

For example, the side could go out and beat Leeds United 6-0 one week to give the Old Trafford crowd something to savour. But when those same fans trooped back in the following week they could only watch in bewilderment as their side succumbed 5-1. Admittedly to a very fine Tottenham Hotspur side who would finish the campaign in third place behind champions Burnley and runners-up Wolves, and who the following year went on to achieve something United just failed to do – win the first League and Cup Double of the century.

Yet Roy Collins remembers that the emphasis on youth was still there and the youth team was still impressive. He used to watch their matches and saw many of the players who would later be a force learning their trade. One player in particular stands out. "There was a buzz going around that United had signed a young Irish lad called George Best and what he could do had to be seen. When I went to see him in a youth game he didn't look five stone wet through but once he started playing he was as good as everybody said. Even then we knew he was a star of the future."

Another new recruit around this time was a signing from Celtic who would be a key figure at Old Trafford for the best part of a decade. Paddy Crerand joined United for £56,000 in 1963 and combined a strong physical presence at wing-half with superb passing skills and great vision. After nearly 400 games with the club he joined the coaching staff before a brief spell as manager at Northampton Town.

In the FA Cup in 1960, memories of Munich came flooding back as the fifth round paired United with Sheffield Wednesday, their opponents in the same competition that marked the first match after the disaster. The Yorkshire side were to gain their revenge on the same Old Trafford stage, winning 1-0 after half-back Maurice Setters conceded a penalty.

The following season saw a poor start to the campaign, with the side third from bottom of the table at the beginning of October, after only two wins in 11 games though they were both comprehensive results with Everton going down 4-0 and West Ham United 6-1 on their visits to Old Trafford.

Busby took action to remedy the goals being conceded by bringing Shay Brennan from midfield to right-back. Brennan made his debut in the cauldron that was the fifth-round FA Cup match against Sheffield Wednesday in the first match after the Munich disaster. He had been at the club since joining as a 16-year-old in 1953 and would play more than 350 games for United as well as winning 19 Republic of Ireland caps. The highlight of his career was winning a European Cup winners' medal in 1968.

Results improved and, on New Year's Eve, United had the satisfaction of a 5-1 win in the Manchester derby with Alex Dawson netting a hat-trick. There were other results, though, that gave the fans far less pleasure. United suffered a 6-0 reverse against Leicester City with a debutant in goal. Ronnie Briggs, 17, was given his place because of injury to Harry Gregg and it was to be a tough baptism. It proved his only League game of the season.

United also lost 5-1 to Sheffield Wednesday who, again, also proved their nemesis in the FA Cup defeating them 7-2 at Old Trafford in a replayed fourth-round Cup-tie after United had travelled to Yorkshire and earned a 1-1 draw. If United's performance in the season was the subject of a school report it would read 'good, but must do better'. With a seventh place finish in the League, Busby himself knew there was still work to be done.

The 1961-62 campaign was worse for the club and saw United finish in 15th position, although there was a good Cup run to raise the spirits of the supporters. Bolton Wanderers and Arsenal were both accounted for before the fickle hand of fate again drew Sheffield Wednesday out of the hat. The game at Old Trafford was drawn, but it was a successful foray across the Pennines for a 2-0 win. A win over Preston North End with a 2-1 home win in a replay booked a semi-final place against holders Spurs at Hillsborough, Sheffield. Here, though, the Reds were comfortably eclipsed 3-1.

The spectre of relegation came to haunt Old Trafford the following year as the team hit a slump. There were only a dozen wins all season thinly spread among a fixture list containing 20 defeats. In October there was a 6-2 defeat away to Spurs and Burnley, Ipswich

Town and Nottingham Forest all scored five against United during the season. In the end the Reds escaped relegation by three points and it was their neighbours across the city who finished below them and had to endure Second Division football.

Despite the poor showing in the League, the team that would in time stride the European stage was now beginning to be put in place. The likes of Nobby Stiles and Tony Dunne had forced their way into the first team. The arrival of David Herd from Arsenal for £35,000 brought a proven goalscorer to Old Trafford. He had been second to Jimmy Greaves as the Division One leading scorer in 1960-61 and netted 144 times for the club in 262 appearances until he moved to Stoke City in the summer of 1968.

Although the season brought Cup glory, Charlton remembers there was also a threat of relegation. He is honest to admit the team struggled and the cause was not helped by the long break from football caused by the severe winter that disrupted football for weeks, although he believes the team was better than its final League position suggests and that the threat of relegation was never really serious.

David Gaskell beats Everton's Alex Young to the ball at Old Trafford in April 1962. Less than 32,000 saw a 1-1 draw.

If the season had been an aberration, the basis of a great side was now in place. For the fans there was the consolation of a trip to Wembley and the knowledge that it would not be long before the new side assembled by Busby would bring its rewards in the League. They would not have long to wait and the triumvirate of Charlton, Law and Best would soon be staking their place in football history.

A Prophecy Fulfilled

MATT Busby's judgment in footballing matters was usually spot on and when, in the wake of the Munich disaster he predicted it would be five years before Manchester United would be back, his judgement was duly vindicated. The team had struggled in the League, but would find glory at Wembley.

The harsh winter that year had seriously affected the season's fixture programme and United didn't play a match between late December 1962 and late February 1963. Suddenly when football was back the Reds found themselves with four FA Cup-ties in one action-packed month.

On 4 March, Huddersfield Town were swept away 5-0 at Old Trafford and a week later Aston Villa were the visitors to be despatched by a single goal. Five days later Chelsea made the journey north and succumbed 2-1. The first away draw saw United travel to Coventry City and triumph 3-1 to set up a semi-final tie against Southampton to be played at Villa Park, Birmingham. A 1-0 win was enough to secure a trip to Wembley.

Leicester City had finished fourth in the table and had won plaudits for their attractive style of football. United had just escaped relegation. Yet somehow the role of underdog didn't sit too easily on their star packed line-up. So it proved as United controlled the game from the start in what was the Football Association's centenary year.

Afterwards Busby singled out Denis Law and Pat Crerand for special praise in an impressive team display that gave the lie to the League performances of the season. And it was those two who combined for the opening goal after half an hour. Leicester goalkeeper Gordon Banks saved a Bobby Charlton shot, but his throw out was intercepted by Crerand, who beat two defenders before sending over a cross. Law took the ball, feigned to make space and wrong-foot two defenders and his right-foot shot on the turn beat Banks. Law still jokes: "I can still see that pass coming towards me."

Mike Kelly had been to every home and away game and secured his Cup Final ticket, but was unable to afford the transport down to the capital, so he set off on the Friday to hitch hike to Wembley. He was lucky when two former school friends driving down for the Final picked him up.

He concurs with the view that Law had been man of the match. "To be honest deep down I didn't think we would win because we had struggled that season, but Law played better than anyone could have expected. He played them off the park. The way United performed that day it was quickly obvious there was no way we were going to lose."

Law earned the name of 'The King' during a long and illustrious career at Old Trafford following his arrival for another British record fee. Matt Busby was never afraid to raid the United coffers and, just as Albert Quixall had been a record signing before him, Law now generated headlines for himself and the club when £115,000 brought him back from Torino in Italy where he had moved to in 1961 when Manchester City sold him for £100,000.

Denis Law is beaten by Leicester City's Ritchie Norman during the 1963 FA Cup Final.

Born in Aberdeen, Law had joined Huddersfield Town in 1955 where he came under the guidance of a manager who was also to go on to greater things. Bill Shankly is said to have built up the thin figure of Law by sending him to a local café for steak and milk. Shortly after Shankly made his move to Anfield and a place in football history, Law moved to Manchester, but to Maine Road and a short but successful career with the Sky Blues before the Continent beckoned. The Scotland international was not happy in Italy, but was to get plenty of experience of European football in the red shirt of United in the years ahead.

His goal in the Cup Final underlined a fine first season for the Reds that saw him finish as the top goalscorer. The following year he did even better finishing with 46 goals in all matches and was crowned European Footballer of the Year for 1964. In total he scored 236 goals in 399 appearances for the club. Yet for many United fans the goal they remember Law for came after Busby's reign when his backheel playing for Manchester City consigned United to the Second Division in 1974. Not even the most ardent fan on the terraces though could direct taunts at a man who was synonymous with the glory days of

Manchester United. He was just as passionate for Scotland scoring 30 goals in 55 appearances.

He was a major force in the Cup Final where United were playing at a higher tempo than Leicester and controlled the first half but, although both Johnny Giles and Law again went close, the score remained 1-0 at the break. After the restart it was more of the same and when Giles passed to Charlton, whose well-hit shot was half-saved by Banks, David Herd was on hand to score and it looked a long way back for Leicester.

To their credit they rallied and a diving header by centre-forward

David Herd (no. 9) scores his team's second goal, as teammate Denis Law runs in to support him in the 1963 FA Cup Final against Leicester.

Ken Keyworth in the 80th minute brought them back into contention. Five minutes later, though, and it was all over. Banks might have been a world class goalkeeper, but this had not been one of his better days. He spilled a cross by Giles and it was again Herd who was on hand to take advantage and fire the ball home.

An excited spectator was David Sadler who had joined the club during the season and he recalls he choose Manchester United despite offers from other clubs because they had a reputation for producing and bringing on young players. There were no financial inducements or any sort of bidding war with rival clubs. He was aware of stories of the Busby Babes and the Munich air crash, but his main reason for signing was that he thought he would get his best chance to progress as a player with the club.

Sadler remembers, though, that although Manchester United had a wonderful reputation, the season he arrived was not a good one. "We were struggling and fighting relegation. I was playing A-team and reserve-team games but it was a tense time at Old Trafford. Fortunately by the time of the Cup Final we were safe in the League and, along with the supporters, it was the chance to enjoy the trip to Wembley. Given the season we had had, the Cup was a real bonus and for a young player to travel down to London with the club party was a great experience. I didn't get anywhere near the players but that didn't matter. It was an excellent Final and what a great time we had in London. I'd hardly been at United and here I was at the Cup Final. It was a nice little starter to my career."

Fan Kevin Smith was 14 at the time and had the necessary tokens for a Cup Final ticket, but his dad and elder brother and a few of their friends decided they wanted to make a weekend of it in London. They did not need a youngster along and so his ticket went to one of their friends.

Smith, now 53, recalls: "I went and queued up for the ticket and then couldn't go. I was as sick as a dog. I'd known since after the semi-final that I wouldn't be going because they wanted to go drinking in London and it was too long for me to be left sat in the car with a packet of crisps. It all seemed very unfair but it made me determined that when I was older nothing would stop me going to games. Instead I watched it at home on television. I didn't think the game was a classic, but it was a good win."

As a 13-year-old, Peter Beetham watched the game with his dad on the television and thrilled at the win, then went out to join friends in the local park where they held their own 'Cup Final' with competition to be 'Manchester United' fierce as they lived not far from the ground. "I'd been going to matches regularly and used to go to The Cliff to watch the players train and get their autographs for my scrapbooks. Like all the youngsters supporting United I had got caught up in the whole atmosphere of the Cup. Everybody was talking about the match and it was a great time."

It was the fourth time Busby had taken United to Wembley and the second time he had seen his team lift the trophy. The trips to Wembley in 1957 and 1958 had both ended in controversial defeat. For two United players in particular this moment was special. Bobby Charlton and Bill Foulkes had collected losers' medals in both matches. Now they could enjoy the atmosphere as they went to collect their winners' medals.

Foulkes was one of the great unsung heroes of United, yet his record is impressive. As well as playing in United's two losing FA Cup Finals he would go on to win four Championship winners' medals and, at the age of 36, was an integral part of the European Cup-winning team in 1968. As a Munich survivor he bridged the gap between the Busby Babes of the 1950s and the European Cup-winning side of the 1960s. Not surprisingly, in a player who was around so long, he was solid and consistent in defence.

When he signed for United at 18 Foulkes still worked part-time in the Lancashire coalfields and while he worked his way through the ranks at Old Trafford he continued as a miner. Perhaps surprisingly he won only one England cap, but what he achieved on the domestic front more than compensated. During his 18 years as a professional with the Reds he appeared in more than 600 games at full-back and centre-half before retiring in 1970.

The other player from the two 1950s Finals, Charlton remembers: "They went into the Final favourites against Manchester United, but on the day we outplayed them. We certainly didn't look like a team that was supposedly at one stage in danger of relegation. Denis Law had come into the team and he was a really exciting player. The type people expected of Manchester United. We had some strong players and it was a convincing win.

"The Cup is always exciting because it is a showpiece and the Wembley surface is superb. The whole day was magical. It was a warm day and the sun was shining and we had a good team. I felt I played really well. Earlier in the season Spurs had beaten us at home and Jimmy Greaves had asked me whether we would win the Cup and even then I said yes, there was no doubt. It was the first time for a while that United had won something and it was a good time."

As a former Manchester United and Leicester City player, Johnny Morris had divided loyalties and invitations from both clubs to go to the after-match function. He hit upon a simple solution to the dilemma of which to attend. "I decided to go to the banquet of whichever side won because the atmosphere would be better with the winners."

The game itself was not a classic but Morris singled out the performance of Paddy Crerand as the man of the match. He also holds the controversial view that the Cup Final win saved Busby's job. "United were struggling in the League that season and flirted with relegation. However much a hero Matt Busby was at Old Trafford, United were a club that demanded success and there hadn't been too much of that recently. Winning the Cup took the pressure off."

As he watched the game his mind returned to his own Cup Final success in 1948. The magic of Wembley was still there and he knew exactly what it felt like for the Manchester United players following in the footsteps of the last side to lift the trophy.

Skipper Noel Cantwell (top) keeps a tight grip on the FA Cup as he is chaired by his teammates after Leicester were beaten at Wembley.

He explained: "Wembley was always a good day out. Every foot-baller wants to play there and, because the ground was only used for the Cup Final or internationals, not many got the chance. Having League play-offs and such like in the stadium's later years took some of the edge off the experience, but in 1963 it was still special. Also, all the grounds in our day were muddy and carved up with week-in-week-out football, but the Wembley pitch was perfect and provided the perfect opportunity to play good football."

Morris was now in non-League football, where his career was coming to a close, and the trip to Wembley brought an unforeseen benefit. While chatting to the Leicester directors he met a friend of one who offered him a job. It is a measure of how little footballers of his day earned that, once it was time to hang up his boots, a decent day job had to be found. For the next 19 years he would work selling tyres while also being involved in non-League football as a manager.

The League season may have been a disappointing one but the fans were willing to forgive and forget in the wake of a Cup triumph that saw them back to winning ways after the horrors of Munich. The 300,000 people who lined the streets to welcome their heroes home were cheering more than an FA Cup win. They were celebrating the rehabilitation of a club. United were back and the future looked more than rosy. It looked positively red.

Busby himself was quick to recognise the important role the supporters had played in the side's recovery. He wanted them to enjoy this winning moment and he was convinced there would be more glory for them to share in. He was right, of course.

United Win the Title

THE third of the great sides built by Matt Busby was now reaching the peak of its powers with the personnel who were to become household names not just in this country, but across the footballing world now in place and ready to take their place in the pantheon of football's greats.

If the 1963-64 season was one where Manchester United fell just short of honours the following year was to make amends. This was the seventh full season since the Munich disaster and the rebuilding of the side was now complete. The Reds were again League champions.

The previous year saw United finish runners-up in the League and reach the semi-finals of the Cup. It also saw the debut of a young man from Belfast. Three days before the 1963 Cup Final George Best turned 17 and was offered a professional contract by Busby. His move from the ground staff to being a potent force in the United side would be swift. It did not take long in the 1963-64 season for him to make his first-team debut, taking his bow in a 1-0 win over West Bromwich Albion at Old Trafford on 14 September 1963.

David Sadler also made his League debut, in place of David Herd, in the 1963-64 season. But eventually it was as a centre-half, rather than the inside-forward or centre-forward positions he played in his younger days, that he made his mark at Old Trafford. "I'd no real expectations of making the first team and was just hoping to get into the Reserves on a regular basis, but in the Charity Shield we had taken a bit of a hiding in losing to Everton 4-0 and when the team sheet went up for the first League game of the season, away to Sheffield Wednesday, I was down to play and it was incredible. I remember looking at the sheet and it was all a bit of a blur in my mind."

Like all players his League debut was special, and like many he was carried along on a tide of adrenaline and emotion and details later are sketchy as the time raced by. "It was an incredible match. I was playing centre-forward and up against me was Peter Swan, who had recently been the England centre-half. I remember at one point midway through the second half I broke clear and was about to go one-on-one with the goalkeeper when Swan hacked me down and instead of scoring my first goal I was chewing dirt. Afterwards I think I was a little surprised that after comparatively few games in United's junior sides I had managed to hold my own in the First Division. I played a dozen games before Herd came back"

He recalls that by this stage the major rebuilding was well under way at the club and Busby's potent mix of promising young players allied to major signings was starting to take effect. Old hands like Maurice Setters, Bill Foulkes and Noel Cantwell had been joined by Denis Law and the youngsters breaking through alongside Sadler

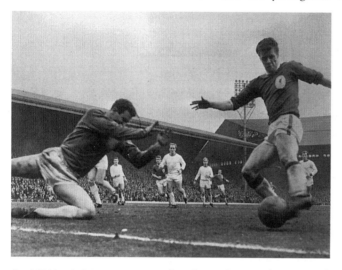

April 1964 at Anfield and Alf Arrowsmith's shot is about to be smothered by Harry Gregg. United lost 3-0 and ended the season runners-up, four points behind the Merseysiders.

included George Best and Nobby Stiles. There was a general gelling together of a side that would go on to greater glory.

It was a happy mixture and Sadler recalls there was always help and advice. Before his debut the senior players had helped to calm his nerves. The Reds still had an impressive youth side, which Sadler and Best were both part of and won the FA Youth Cup in 1964.

Another player who arrived after Munich but would be a key figure in the 1960s success was the Irish full-back Tony Dunne. He had joined United from the Dublin club Shelbourne United and made his debut in 1960 and would remain at Old Trafford for 13 years as a first-team player making over 500 first-team appearances. The 1964-65 campaign saw him win one of his two Championship medals, the second coming two years later when he would also go on to win European Cup honours. He was capped 32 times by Ireland and, after leaving United in 1973, he played five seasons with Bolton Wanderers before finishing his playing career in the USA.

As has been mentioned, the season saw United challenging for the title and making a spirited defence of their FA Cup, but they were to fall just short on both counts. There was also a return to Europe as the Reds entered the European Cup-winners' Cup, but more of their Continental excursions later.

Busby had never been one to tolerate too much dissent from his players as Johnny Morris had discovered. Soon another talented player would be heading out of Old Trafford after falling out with the manager once too often, in an incident that had echoes of the Morris affair of 15 years or so earlier. This time the player to depart was Johnny Giles who went to Leeds for a £37,500 fee after six years with the club. There, of course, his career was to prosper but, with the talent at their disposal, United could afford the loss and there could only be one boss at Old Trafford.

In the title race United were vying with Liverpool and on 4 April a visit to Anfield looked set to be the crucial fixture. A 3-0 defeat effectively ended the title race baring a major slip up by the Merseysiders and they went on to win the title by four points from United.

The game against West Bromwich Albion on 18 January 1964 was an important first in the annals of Manchester United. On this day Bobby Charlton, Denis Law and George Best played together for the first time. Injuries and a suspension for Law after a sending-off against Aston Villa in November had put off the date with destiny, and the three instantly struck up an accord with Charlton at centre-forward, Law at inside-left and Best on the left wing.

The West Brom defenders would not be the last to learn that such a combination was hard to contain when they hit form. United won 4-1 and all three got on the scoresheet with Law bagging a couple. The goal that had the fans talking as they poured from the ground, though, was the strike by Best. When the Irishman collected the ball from Law he went wide of the defenders and then shot from a seemingly impossible angle only for the ball to find a gap inside the post. Such footballing magic would captivate the fans in the coming years.

In the FA Cup United reached the semi-finals, but to do so they needed to come through a marathon sixth-round tie against Second Division Sunderland. At Old Trafford, United were 3-1 down with the clock showing only four minutes remaining when Charlton fired home a Best corner. With time ticking away, Best brought the sides level and ensured a replay.

In the replay 68,000 fans packed into Roker Park hopeful of seeing the League's high flyers brought down to earth and it was Sunderland who, again, opened the scoring with a goal late in the first half. Law ensured the game went to extra-time, but Sunderland, belying the gulf between the two, again took the lead. It needed another Houdini-style escape as Charlton scored on the stroke of time.

Five days later the two teams met again at a neutral venue, Leeds Road, Huddersfield. This time United showed their true form and Sunderland were swept aside. Even so it was the North East side who took the lead early in the second half. This time a goal only spurred the Reds to life and parity was restored within 60 seconds as Law pounced on a David Herd shot that had rebounded off a defender. Four more goals followed as United posted a 5-1 win and Law collected his hat-trick. All the goals came within a 15-minute blitz that ensured a semi-final place.

Having had the rub of the green to get past Sunderland, there was a feeling on the terraces that this was going to be United's year for the Cup. Such is the nature of the competition that for a team to reach Wembley there has to be an element of luck and United appeared to be riding theirs. It was not to be, however. West Ham, captained by Bobby Moore, were well in control, winning 3-1 at Hillsborough, Sheffield. West Ham went on to win the Cup and the following year enjoyed success in Europe when they lifted the European Cup-winners' Cup with a team born entirely in England.

Busby now had a settled side and money was diverted to improve the facilities at Old Trafford with £320,000 being spent to bring the ground up to standard as a venue for the 1966 World Cup. The new north stand would seat 10,500 fans and have terracing for 10,000 more. It would make United's home the envy of most of the League, but at a price as the club went into debt to build it.

As a young supporter Peter Beetham remembers that with a crowd of school friends they would go at lunch time and wander around the building site as the work went on to transform the ground. "The development would make the ground one of the most impressive in the country and we were captivated watching the new stand going up piece by piece. There was not much concern with health and safety because there used to be a crowd of us kids stood eating our chips as the work went on around us."

Lifelong fan Bill Makin had started watching United when they shared a home with Manchester City at Maine Road, in the early years after the war. He used to go every week and watch both clubs. As the new stadium took shape it renewed his belief that both clubs would have been better having one stadium that would have been a showpiece for the city and a Wembley of the north. Even today the idea still appeals and there are examples on the Continent with the Milan clubs AC Milan and Inter sharing the San Siro stadium.

Having no money to spend on players was, for the moment, not such a burden. The heart of the team that would go on to lift the European Cup was now in place. Charlton, Best and Law were gelling as a unit. The full-backs Shay Brennan and Tony Dunne were established. Bill Foulkes had cemented his place at centre-half and a young Nobby Stiles was making himself a regular fixture at half-back. Paddy Crerand was the other half-back and David Sadler was starting to be a regular in the starting line-up.

However formidable the side seemed on paper they didn't start the 1964-65 campaign like champions. There was just one win in their first six games, a 3-1 win over the Cup holders West Ham at Old Trafford. For the next 14 games though the only points United let slip was a draw at Burnley's Turf Moor ground. The most impressive result was a 7-0 win over Aston Villa in which Law collected four and David Herd two, with a single goal for John Connelly. United were up with the challengers for League glory.

The main contenders as 1965 dawned were Leeds United and Chelsea and the challenge of the London side was already faltering when they arrived at Old Trafford in March and were on the receiv-

Denis Law is delighted. George Best's shot has just found the West Ham net at Old Trafford in September 1964. Over 45,000 saw United win 3-1. They went on to win the League championship.

ing end of a 4-0 drubbing. It was part of an impressive run-in to the season's close that saw the Reds lose only one in 11 games. Another key result was the visit to face Leeds at Elland Road where United won thanks to the only goal of the game scored by Connelly.

It was a nail-biting finish to the campaign. Leeds headed the table with 60 points and one game to play. United were a point behind with two games left. Leeds also had the additional pressure of an FA Cup Final against Arsenal, who were United's opponents in the penultimate match of the season.

Leeds had been United's nemesis in the FA Cup in a game that was shrouded in controversy. It was the Reds fourth consecutive appearance in an FA Cup semi-final and the games with Leeds turned into a battle. The worst incident before a 65,000 crowd at Hillsborough saw Law and Jackie Charlton involved in a wrestling match. There were other flare-ups with punches thrown and players squaring up to each other. The match itself ended a goalless draw.

The replay at Nottingham was a tough encounter but without some of the worst excesses of the previous game. A late goal for Leeds ensured it was the Yorkshire club who would be Wembley bound and it was another disappointment for the Reds. To make matters worse one of their fans attacked the referee, which ensured the football would be eclipsed in the following day's papers.

Versatile winger John Connelly, a member of England's victorious 1966 World-Cup winning squad. He won League championship medals with Burnley and United.

Back with the League, it was a Monday night when Leeds played their away fixture at Birmingham, while United faced Arsenal. United cruised to a comfortable victory 3-1 against a side with Wembley on their minds. What was holding the spectators spellbound though was the tannoy announcements from the Birmingham-Leeds game. The Yorkshire side had to win to force the title to be decided with United's final game of the season away to Aston Villa. In the Midlands it was turning into an epic tussle with, first, Birmingham taking the lead and then Leeds fighting back. The news came though that the game was drawn 3-3. United were champions although defeat at Villa ensured the title was only theirs on goal-average.

David Sadler played only six League games and it was not enough to earn a Championship-winning medal. He was still being played at centre-forward, but David Herd played for the bulk of the season. He remembers: "I never quite established myself at centre-forward and although I missed out on what was a successful season I was never too disappointed because I was still only 18 and my breakthrough into the first-team squad had happened so quickly. George by that time was really flying." And that could only be good news for Manchester United.

In Search of the Holy Grail

THE Munich disaster had not destroyed Matt Busby's love affair with European football or dented his ambition to produce Manchester United sides that could compete with the Continent's best. For him, winning the European Cup remained the Holy Grail and the events of 6 February 1958 had turned that ambition into an obsession.

Busby admitted, many years later, that he had undergone considerable soul-searching. That he had been instrumental in ensuring that English clubs took their place in European competition and that had indirectly led to the catastrophic consequences for the team he had built, weighed heavily on his mind. In the end he concluded, rightly, that there had really been no alternative.

United were nearly back in the competition in 1958-59 despite finishing only ninth the previous season. There were calls echoed throughout Europe that because of the disaster a special exception should be made to allow the Reds to compete. It was though to be scuppered by officialdom back home.

Busby had had his disputes with the sport's ruling bodies. Not least in his determination to take his team into Europe when the view of the Football League was that England's champion side should withdraw from the event. Whether this was a case of settling scores or not will never be known. The facts of the case, though, are not in dispute.

Having received the invitation from UEFA, the body responsible for the European Cup, United were keen to play and had the support of the Football Association. The Football League, though, made clear their opposition and despite recourse to appeals procedures it was the Football League who prevailed. They successfully argued that it was a tournament for champion clubs and United were not the English League champions.

The Reds were in the wilderness years as far as European football was concerned, although there was a chance in October 1960 to get a brief taste of what they were missing out on when Real Madrid played a friendly at Old Trafford and 51,000 fans saw the Spanish side, led by the great Alfredo Di Stefano, win 3-2. The game fulfilled a promise that Real had made in the wake of the Munich crash that the five-times European Cup winners would play at Old Trafford and make no charge for their presence.

United's return proper came in the 1963-64 season courtesy of their FA Cup triumph over Leicester City. It was one of the highlights of the Cup triumph for Busby that he was now able to bring European opposition to Old Trafford. His view that English teams could only improve by meeting the best in Europe had not been diminished and such competitions provided the ideal opportunity.

David Sadler believes that because Manchester United were so imbued with the idea of European football and, because, from first joining he was seeing games against Continental sides and was travelling abroad, it provided valuable experience for the European Cup campaign in 1968. The Munich disaster was never discussed among the players and certainly not mentioned in front of the two survivors in the side, Bobby Charlton and Bill Foulkes.

But he adds: "Although people didn't talk about the great team that had perished, the Busby Babes side were a presence. They were a part of the club and that took on a greater importance as we progressed in European competitions. When we won the European Cup it was like the end of a crusade, but taking part in the Inter-Cities Fairs Cup in my first full season at the club was an important step along the way."

United's first opponents were the Dutch Second Division club Willem II and it was not the happiest of returns for United. Within ten minutes they were a goal down and the Reds made hard work of overcoming a spirited side. David Herd scored an equaliser, but blotted his copybook when he was sent off with ten minutes of the game remaining for a bad foul. The Dutch side could claim to have been unlucky not to have been credited with a goal when the ball appeared to go under goalkeeper Harry Gregg, but the match finished a draw.

In the return United made no mistake as they cruised to a 6-1 victory with a performance that included a hat-trick for Denis Law. The next round pitted the Reds against the Cup holders Tottenham Hotspur in an all-English tie that neither team wanted, but the fans relished. In the opening leg, at White Hart Lane, Spurs scored twice to give themselves a valuable lead to take to Old Trafford. Cliff Jones and Dave Mackay combined down the left for the opener scored by the Scotland international Mackay and a mistake by Tony Dunne, whose pass to the goalkeeper was intercepted by Terry Dyson, gifted the second in the closing minutes.

Spurs' hopes in the second leg suffered a blow early on when Mackay went into a tackle with United's Noel Cantwell and was clearly badly injured. Cantwell hurriedly called for a stretcher as the Spurs man lay prone. He had suffered a double fracture of his left leg and the London side were down to ten men. They battled heroically, but to no avail. Jimmy Greaves scored for the visitors but two goals for Bobby Charlton with less than 15 minutes played, and a brace for David Herd, booked United's passage to the next round.

Sporting Club Lisbon were the opponents and the two ties proved high-scoring affairs. At Old Trafford, United triumphed 4-1, with the prolific Denis Law scoring a hat-trick although two of his goals came courtesy of penalties. If anything the scoreline did not do United justice as they looked worth more goals. Still, for the fans it seemed that a three-goal advantage would be enough. That, though, was a dangerous underestimation of their opponents on home turf.

The date 18 March would enter the annals of Manchester United Football Club as the day they suffered their worst-ever defeat in Europe, when they collapsed to a 5-0 drubbing that did not unduly flatter the Portuguese.

The omens were not good as early as the second minute when Dunne conceded a penalty for handball. It was 2-0 to Sporting at half-time and three goals in the opening nine minutes of the second half wrapped up the tie. The European Cup-winners' Cup would not be staying in England.

Busby, normally not one for expletives and throwing teacups in the dressing-room, was furious with the players, believing the lead earned at Old Trafford should have been enough to take United into the semi-finals. Following the struggle to rebuild after Munich he raged that the chance to make a mark in Europe again had been squandered in such a fashion. To make matters worse, a handful of players went on a late-night drinking session and were to incur Busby's wrath as a result. His damning verdict was that the team had let down themselves, him and the people of Manchester.

An away win at Spurs in the League the following Saturday helped improve his mood and the threatened fines never materialised. Busby even apologised for losing his temper. For United the return to Europe was over for that year, but the following season saw the club back enjoying Continental football courtesy of a runners-up spot in

Division One. This time they were to participate in the Inter-Cities Fairs Cup in the 1964-65 season.

As we have seen this was a busy and productive season for United on the domestic front as they won the League title and reached the semi-finals of the FA Cup. They also enjoyed some success on foreign fields. Their first opponents were the Swedish side, Djurgårdens IF, and before a crowd of only 6,537 they were held to a 1-1 draw with Herd scoring the goal for the Reds with the clock ticking down. The return, though, was decidedly easier with United running out 6-1 winners and the goal machine that was Law again notching up a hat-trick.

With the attacking potential United possessed courtesy of Best, Charlton and Law any side could be ripped apart if they caught the Reds on a good day. Borussia Dortmund did just that and matched the Swedes in succumbing 6-1 and that was playing the opening tie in Germany. This time it was Charlton who netted the hat-trick and ensured that the second leg in Manchester would be a formality. Busby described it as the best performance in Europe for many years against a side that had reached the European Cup semi-final the previous year. There was no way back for the Germans and a 4-0 win at Old Trafford ensured a handsome 10-1 aggregate victory.

Just as they had the previous year in European competition United again drew an English side. This time Everton were the opposition and it proved a close-run affair. The Liverpool side travelled to Old Trafford and opened the scoring only for John Connelly to restore parity. It ensured the second leg would be a difficult hurdle for the Reds to negotiate, but they travelled to Goodison and progressed to the next round thanks to a 2-1 win.

A 5-0 win on the road against RC Strasbourg virtually guaranteed a semi-final place for United. The return leg was goalless but the Reds were still comfortably through to the next round where their semi-final opponents were Ferencvaros and the Hungarians showed they would be no pushovers. United managed to win 3-2, but there was doubts a one-goal advantage would be enough in Budapest. A penalty for the home side after Nobby Stiles was somewhat harshly penalised for handball meant the aggregate score was level. A coin was tossed to see who would have home advantage and United lost so it was back to Budapest. It had been a long season for United and it was now the middle of June, which might have explained their 2-1 defeat before a 60,000 crowd.

Nobby Stiles has since said of the season that it was in this Fairs Cup campaign that United hit their richest form with the standard of football they played and the goals that were scored. In the end he felt that it was the length of the season that took its toll. Players today might complain about the amount of football they play but that year Stiles played 66 games, including international duty with the England Under-23s.

However, winning the League title ensured that United were back in Europe and this time in the all-important European Cup. With a side that was hitting its peak Busby and Jimmy Murphy believed that this represented the best chance of bringing the trophy back to Old Trafford. In the preliminary round against the Finnish amateurs HJK Helsinki, United had the best possible start with David Herd scoring in less than a minute. By half-time it was 3-1 and, although Helsinki pulled a goal back, it was a confident Reds side that emerged at Old Trafford for the second leg and comfortably dispatched the visitors 6-0 with Connelly scoring a hat-trick and two goals for Best.

The East German Army team, ASK Vorwaerts, were the opponents in the next round and it meant a trip to Berlin and through Checkpoint Charlie to play the tie. In driving sleet and on a frozen pitch United won 2-0 courtesy of two late goals for Law and Connelly. In the second leg an early goal for Herd ensured there would be no way back for the Germans and the Reds ran out 3-1 winners with Herd getting a hat-trick. The draw now pitted the Manchester side against formidable opposition in the shape of Portuguese side Benfica, who had been European Cup Finalists in four of the previous five seasons, and had won the competition twice.

A 64,000 crowd at Old Trafford were regally entertained with the visit of one of the top teams in Europe who boasted among their ranks the great Eusebio. The visitors opened the scoring, but goals from Law and Herd ensured a half-time lead, which was further extended with a Bill Foulkes header. The United cause suffered a setback, though, when the Portuguese side scored to limit the Reds advantage to one goal.

Benfica were unbeaten on their own ground in European competition, but that record was to be shattered in stunning fashion by Manchester United who routed them 5-1. The Reds were three goals in front after only 14 minutes, with two goals for Best and one for Connelly. Best's first was a header from a Tony Dunne free-kick while the second saw goalkeeper Gregg launch a huge goal-kick that was headed on to the Irishman by Herd. Best beat two players before rifling a shot home. The 75,000 crowd were stunned by the display. A Shay Brennan own-goal gave the home side a glimmer of hope but it was soon extinguished with second half goals for Paddy Crerand and Charlton. The Portuguese newspapers dubbed Best, 'El Beatle'.

Busby said afterwards that Best had destroyed the opposition. He had also failed to follow instructions. The plan was for United to play it tight for the first 20 minutes. When Best was in such a mood, though, tactics tended to go out of the window. The player himself reflecting on his performance some time later was at a loss to explain it. There was only one word that summed it up and that was 'genius'.

United were now favourites to win the European Cup and their opponents in the semi-finals were FK Partizan Belgrade. In the first leg in Belgrade, Best played but was carrying an injury and it flared up during the match greatly limiting his influence. Partizan showed they were a better side than people had perhaps given them credit for and with the Reds as a whole putting in a below par performance the home side finished the night 2-0 winners though Law had twice hit the bar for United.

Back at Old Trafford Partizan defended well and United struggled to break them down. Pat Crerand and Mihaslovic were sent off for fighting and United's only goal of the night came from Nobby Stiles whose cross was palmed into the net by the Partizan goalkeeper. Manchester United were out of the competition and for Busby it was a particularly low point. He feared his ambition of winning the European Cup would now never be realised.

Sir Bobby Charlton recalls: "It was disappointing because we felt we had a good team. There was a sense among some that perhaps our chance had gone."

His view is echoed by David Sadler who, although he didn't take part in the competition, was a member of the first-team squad. He also believes this was the year the Reds should have won the tournament. United had an established side with a good mix of youth and experience. It had been a shock when the semi-final saw the team beaten and many thought the best chance of bringing the trophy to Old Trafford had gone. As Sadler explained, the most successful teams have at best a three- or four-year spell of dominance and at United it was felt the team would now start to break up.

He said: "There is a point where the more experienced players are reaching the end, and the young players in the wings are making the transition from being occasional choices to really performing regularly and it seemed that was the state the 1966 European Cup side was now in, and it would take a little time for the new team to settle. Losing to Partizan Belgrade was the biggest disappointment I had experienced at the club up to then. What made it worse was we knew we had the opportunity to get to the Final and we let it slip through our grasp."

Champions Again

MANCHESTER United did not have to wait long before ensuring another crack at the European Cup as they swept to the title in 1967 playing football that was a match for any of the earlier teams created by Matt Busby. Indeed, after one performance the manager described the football fare produced as his finest hour, though events to come in Europe would soon ensure a finer one.

The Reds had ensured they gained further valuable experience on the Continent the previous season. But they could only finish the League in fourth place. A disappointing campaign for the reigning Champions perhaps, given the high standards they had set themselves, but, as we have seen, there was a magnificent European Cup run that saw them reach the semi-finals, although many felt this had been United's best chance of winning the trophy.

In the League in the 1965-66 season United were consistent without being outstanding. There were too many games drawn that needed to be wins to keep them in contention for the title. In all they won 18 games, but drew 15 more and they finished ten points behind the new Champions Liverpool. It meant, after enjoying European football for the previous three seasons, the 1966-67 campaign would see them with only domestic honours to compete for.

The 1965-66 campaign also brought its almost traditional FA Cup semi-final. This was the fifth successive year United had reached this stage and they had progressed only once, when they won the Cup in 1963. It is said that losing in the semi-finals was the worst of all because Wembley was so near and there was not even the consolation of the memorable day at the Twin Towers that the losing Finalists enjoy. This time Everton were the semi-final opponents and triumphed 1-0 in a game played at Burnden Park.

Bill Makin recalls the frustration for the fans as United seemed to always falter at the final hurdle with Wembley in their sights. Two seasons before he had travelled to Hillsborough to see the side lose to West Ham United and the crowd was so tightly packed in that, as he says: "You couldn't see a thing unless the ball went on the grandstand roof. It was so bad I decided to get out and go and see if I could listen to it on the radio. The bloke on the gate wouldn't let me out because the gates couldn't be opened until 15 minutes from end. I was reminded of that years later with the Hillsborough tragedy."

He was also at Burnden Park and the viewing conditions were, again, far from ideal, but United were all over Everton and the fans were confident of victory. "We were well on top and looked like finally getting back to Wembley. At half-time there was one of these girl marching bands as the entertainment and they went up and down the same bit of pitch. When play resumed there was a moment when the ball was cleared from the Everton half and the United defenders seemed to have it covered until it hit a rut where the band had been marching. It bounced off at an awkward angle and Everton went on and scored the only goal of the game. I've always blamed that band for costing us the semi-final."

Perhaps because they were without the distraction of Europe the Reds stormed to the title in 1966-67. Coupled with which, the domestic Cup competitions did not involve United for too long. After battling so far and not getting to Wembley in previous years this season the side departed early beaten 2-1 in an FA Cup shock by Norwich City, a side that would end the season in mid-table in the Second Division. The Reds' first outing in the League Cup saw them beaten 5-1 by a Blackpool side that would be relegated from the First Division that season. It was three years before United entered the League Cup competition again.

In the League, though, it was a different story. The opening game of the season set the pattern. With 20 minutes gone, United were 5-1 up as they ripped apart the West Brom defence; although the visitors were to claw two goals back to make the final scoreline more respectable. A Boxing Day defeat, 2-1 away to Sheffield United, was the last game United lost in the campaign.

A 20-match undefeated run ensured the League Championship was won with a four-point margin over Nottingham Forest, though the competition had been fierce. Earlier in the season Chelsea had set the pace only to falter, and then Liverpool had headed the challengers at times edging United from their top spot, but all fell back.

While there had been no Championship medal for David Sadler two years before, this season he was to be a regular in the side, play-ing 35 games and winning the coveted medal. It was also during this campaign that he began to play more at centre-half, although he still made most of his appearances at centre-forward that campaign. He recalls: "The conversion to centre-half was just something that seemed to happen as a natural progression. When we finished training we would have a kick-around for 20 minutes and people used to switch positions with defenders having a go as goalscorers and the other way around. There was an under-20s tour to Switzerland which I went on and the centre-half couldn't make it and I stepped in and that was the start of it."

United's supremacy was underlined in the penultimate game of the season when they travelled to West Ham United and ensured the title was theirs with a 6-1 victory. United were 3-0 up after ten minutes as they produced a footballing masterclass. Many of those watching believed that first 30 minutes was as fine a display by a United side as any since the war, although of course there was some stiff competition for that accolade. United had topped the table in March and had not been shifted from the spot. Now Europe beckoned again.

Remembering the West Ham game Sadler recalls: "We knew that if we won we were champions and for me the whole afternoon turned out to be just incredible. We quickly went a couple of goals up and just cruised it. Winning the title was an enormous achievement in itself but all the players were aware that it held the chance of another crack at the European Cup. Even in the moment of victory we knew that was the final mountain for us to climb. It was now a case of onwards and upwards."

The team was largely settled but Busby did add to his squad signing a player who would play a starring role in the European Cup Final. In September 1966 goalkeeper Alex Stepney was signed from Chelsea for £55,000, establishing a new record fee for a goalkeeper. Certainly Busby was satisfied with his signing proclaiming, at the end of the season, that the title would not have been won but for the presence of the young goalkeeper. Stepney made his debut in a Manchester derby soon after he joined and, for the following 12 seasons, he was a regular between the posts for United, completing more than 500 games before he departed to play in the USA in 1978. He won a solitary England cap.

Completing the line-up was winger John Aston. He replaced the experienced John Connelly, 28, an England international and £56,000-signing from Burnley in 1964, who had played more than 100 games for the club, but who was now considered surplus to requirements and was sold to Blackburn Rovers for £40,000.

Aston followed in the path of his father at Old Trafford. John Aston senior was in the 1940s side and won an FA Cup winners' medal in 1948. Aston went one better, winning a European Cup winners' medal when he turned in what many considered was the performance of his career. His first-team career spanned five years until he suffered a broken leg that effectively ended his time at Old Trafford and saw him move to Luton Town in 1972.

Now, in the aftermath of his League Championship triumph, Busby spelt out his priorities, although no one in the club was in any doubt what they were. He now believed he had the squad he needed to make a serious challenge for the European Cup. With time running out for both himself and some of his senior players it was now or never for the ultimate prize.

Charlton remembers: "Law and Best were at their peak and we were scoring a lot of goals. It was a good team. The realisation at the club was always that, to win the European Cup, you first had to win the League. An emotional thing was that, until we won the European Cup, we hadn't done justice to the club's real ambitions. It was a very emotional time."

Bobby Charlton lifts the 1966 European Footballer of the Year trophy.

United, though, still made a decent fist of retaining their League title in the 1967-68 season. Despite the set back of an opening day defeat at the hands of Everton, 3-1 at Goodison, the Reds then went 11 games without defeat. By Boxing Day, United were top of the table with a three-point advantage over their nearest challengers, Liverpool. It seemed the title might be retained but, perhaps distracted by their endeavours in Europe, United's League form faltered. Three defeats in March, to Chelsea, Coventry City and, crucially, a 3-1 reverse in the Manchester derby at Old Trafford, ensured an open contest.

The lead at the top of the table see-sawed in the closing weeks of the season and, with four teams in contention, it was the closest contest for many years. As well as the two Manchester clubs, Liverpool and Leeds United were also challenging. In April there was

a home defeat for United against Liverpool and a calamitous 6-3 reverse against West Brom, which saw Manchester City top the table for the first time in the campaign. In the penultimate game of the season United handed out a 6-0 drubbing to Newcastle United with George Best getting a hat-trick, but it was too late.

With the last game of the season there was only one thing certain; the title would be coming to Manchester. But would it return to Old Trafford or would their great rivals manage to emerge from the Red shadow that had been cast across the city in the Busby era and grab some glory for themselves? City topped the table on goal-average and faced a trip to Newcastle United, where victory would ensure they won the title. United faced a home game against Sunderland.

As the Championship race with Manchester City reached its climax, David Sadler recalls: "The city of Manchester was caught up in the whole excitement of who would win the title. City had been getting together a good side. There was also a feeling that, at that time, Manchester was at the centre of a lot of good that was happening in lots of areas and that included football, and it was a good time to be playing for either United or City. Unfortunately on this occasion City were about to take over, but the great rivalry between the fans never extended to the players."

In the event it proved an anticlimax. United went 2-0 down against the Roker Park side in a bruising encounter and, although George Best netted his 28th goal of the season, that was as close as the Reds got. In the event it didn't matter, because Manchester City won 4-3 at Newcastle. However, the blue side of the city would not have long to celebrate before their achievement was overshadowed by events unfolding on the European stage.

Manchester United's George Best and Denis Law walk out before a match at Tottenham.

Champions of Europe

IN 1968 Matt Busby finally realised his dream when his side won the European Cup on a memorable night at Wembley in a match that went to extra-time. As one newspaper report at the time put it for Manchester United the European Cup had become a crusade of the spirit rather than just a soccer competition.

The march to the Final started simply enough when United faced Hibernians, a part-time team from Malta. Two goals apiece for David Sadler and Denis Law ensured the Reds travelled to the holiday island confident of progressing and, although they were held to a goalless draw, the outcome was never in doubt.

Next up were FK Sarajevo and the away tie again ended without a goal. Although the Yugoslavs resorted to roughhouse tactics, the United players kept their heads. A near-capacity crowd of 62,801 at Old Trafford saw the home side take the lead in the 11th minute when the Sarajevo goalkeeper could not hold on to a George Best header and the ball fell to John Aston.

It was another ill-tempered affair and the Yugoslavs had a player sent-off for kicking Best, although the visitors were incensed by an earlier incident when Best appeared to take a swing at their goalkeeper. Best scored the second and although Sarajevo pulled one back, United were through. There was one last chapter to be played out, though, with an ugly scuffle in the tunnel as the players went off.

There was a three-month gap before the quarter-final when the opponents were the Polish side, Górnik Zabrze. Two goals looked to be a reasonable lead to take to the second leg in Silesia, but conditions of snow and biting cold meant the game would be a particularly tough one.

In the event the Reds turned in a brilliant defensive display in the conditions, and kept the home side to one goal to ensure United's fourth appearance in the European Cup semi-finals.

In the early days of the European Cup, one team had dominated and set standards that the rest of the Continent, including England, aspired to match. Now Real Madrid would be the semi-final opponents and the stage was set for one of the great United performances in the competition. The first leg was played at Old Trafford and, although United had the better of the chances, they could manage only one goal when Best met a John Aston cross with a powerful left-foot shot. Madrid were confident such a slender lead could be overcome in the Santiago Bernabeu stadium

David Sadler recalls: "We were disappointed with the home result against Real Madrid. We felt we should have done better and needed a bigger lead to take over there. The Bernabeu, with between 125,000 and 140,000, people in it – depending which book you read - was an impressive stadium and was a difficult place to play in."

Annette Kelly had borrowed £29 from her brother to buy a package trip to the game that included three nights' accommodation and her flight. She went with a friend from work and it was her first trip abroad. Pictures of her with Matt Busby and Brian Kidd taken by her friend with an Instamatic camera show how relaxed the United team were about meeting the band of fans who had made the journey to support their team.

She said: "It was a great adventure. When we arrived we went straight to the ground where the team were training. Afterwards Busby was giving a press conference at the team hotel and we went and stood at the back of it. Jimmy Murphy was standing at the back and we asked him if we could get a picture with Busby and he said he'd bring him over afterwards and he did."

The Madrid team took a 2-0 lead and although United were back in with a chance when Zocco put through his own net, it was a short lived recovery as the home side scored again to lead 3-1 at the interval. The crowd believed they were witnessing their side's progress to the Final, but they had not counted on a tremendous fightback by the Manchester side. In the dressing-room Busby strove to give his players confidence in their ability to claw the tie back and reminded them that, with the goal from Old Trafford, they were effectively only one goal down.

During the first half Sadler is honest enough to admit that United were, in his words, 'getting stuffed'. "We scored through a freakish own-goal and, although it was only 3-1, it felt like it could be 6-1 they were so in control. It was a hammering and at half-time I think we felt it was going to be a question of how many they would score rather than how we could get back in the game.

"Matt Busby didn't say very much to us. There was not a lot to be said, really. I had been playing a fairly defensive role and I was told to push forward more. The manager told the team 'I don't mind being beaten if you lose as a Manchester United team should lose. You haven't played well, now go out and express yourselves'."

Pushing Sadler into his new role paid dividends when he scored in the 70th minute. "I can remember being amazed by the size of the crowd and the enormous noise they were making. I managed to get a goal and, as I flicked the ball past the goalkeeper, it was as if the crowd was a radio at full blast and in a moment somebody had turned it off. There was a stunned silence."

Such was the manner in which the crowd went quiet, Sadler presumed something had happened more serious than even a goal being scored. It quickly dawned on him, though, that it was indeed the shock of the goal. With the goal from Old Trafford, they were now back on level terms – an outcome that had seemed but a rash hope during the first half.

Kelly and her friend were up in the top tier of the huge stadium with a handful of other fans, and they were unable to make their voices heard in one of the game's great theatres. "On the field we were struggling to make an impact, but then suddenly everything started going right. The team were winning, but we were starting to get worried."

After Sadler's goal the football fates had another hand to play before the game was through. Five minutes later the Reds scored again and it was the unlikely figure of Bill Foulkes who got on the scoresheet. Best had made a run down the right wing and the full-back had made a dash up the middle of the park so that when the ball was crossed he was on hand to sidefoot the ball into the net. United were though to the Final.

Years later Foulkes recalled that he had struggled with injury that season and had only just got back into the team. He still cannot explain why he decided to go forward, when it was so out of character. All he knows is that the goal represents his most precious moment in football.

Certainly Sadler remembers being amazed at his presence in the penalty box. "It was something he never did in the normal course of play. There he was taking a pass and putting it away like a seasoned goalscorer. After that, everything was just a blur as we hung on for the final whistle amidst all the excitement."

For Annette Kelly, though, surrounded by angry Spanish fans, things were starting to get ugly. "After the final whistle I was a bit wary and a group of us were making our way out when one of the United fans was attacked by a Madrid fan who started hitting him. We all got away but then, on the coach to the airport as we came to a road junction, angry fans started throwing stones and we had to lie on the floor."

Benfica were the opponents at Wembley in what would be a tense tussle. Even now, more than 30 years on, those who witnessed it can still vividly remember every moment of the drama that unfolded that night. The save by Alex Stepney from a powerful shot by Eusebio that looked goal-bound, the figure of Busby rousing his tired players before the start of extra-time, the way the United players responded to seize the initiative and become the first English side to win the European Cup.

Sadler recalls: "There was no special training or preparation for the match. Everybody was calm. In the dressing-room before people were trying to do their usual preparation and keep things as normal as possible, even though we obviously knew what a fantastic occasion it was. The closer it got to kick-off all I wanted to do was to get the damn game started. I looked across at George Best and he showed no trace of nerves. He was just going about his business as usual. Nobby Stiles always got ready well in advance of the kick-off but would then walk around wearing nothing but his socks and boots. It was a horrible sight!"

Flitting among the players, offering a few words of advice and encouragement, were Matt Busby and Jimmy Murphy. It was more a gesture than anything else. Sadler revealed that in the moments before the match, few players were in a state to take in what was being said. For Sadler this was his first game at Wembley – the venue had been chosen months before – and he had arrived at the mecca for British footballers in the biggest club game it was possible to take part in.

He remembers: "Unusually, we were playing in blue and some of the players were superstitious about it. It didn't matter to me. When we walked out there was a 100,000 crowd. The majority were supporting us and a huge roar went up as we appeared. That was a real adrenaline boost. Strangely, it is one of the few games I have a strong recollection of. It must have been a good game to watch as well as to play in."

Sadler's role was in a defensive midfield position and he recalls having one or two chances in the game where he should have scored, which would have made extra-time unnecessary. It was the 53rd minute before either defence was breached and it was United who struck first. A Sadler cross found Bobby Charlton, who headed over the goalkeeper into the far corner of the net. Benfica responded and put the Reds under considerable pressure. It paid dividends with nine minutes remaining, when a shot by Jaime Graca from a narrow angle brought the sides level.

United held on for extra-time, but there was one nail-biting moment for the players and fans. Sadler remembers: "There was an horrific moment when Eusebio broke through with not long to go. He was one of the world's great players and, at that moment, it was almost as though time had stood still. He slammed the ball and Alex Stepney saved, and from that moment we just held on for the whistle and the chance to regroup."

Benfica goalkeeper Jose Henrique looks around in despair to see the ball in the net for the opening goal of the 1968 European Cup Final, scored by the celebrating Bobby Charlton (behind post).

Thanks to that Stepney save from Eusebio the Reds chances were still alive. Busby urged his players on to one final effort, telling them to keep possession and start playing football again. Sadler said: "We took advantage of the few minutes we had, although I don't remember feeling particularly tired. Matt was going around saying we had won the match and now had to go and win it again. He urged us to keep playing. People were saying things to boost you up but what was said didn't really sink in. Whatever it was worked because quickly into the start of extra-time we scored two goals and they were finished."

Indeed, the Reds scored twice in two minutes. Best dribbled past some dazed defenders and the goalkeeper for the first; and, on his 19th birthday, Brian Kidd scored the next when he headed a Sadler cross, only for it to be blocked, but he made no mistake with the second header. Charlton wrapped up proceedings with his second and United's fourth.

For Kidd it marked a dream start to a United career. In 1966 he had joined the team he supported as a local schoolboy and the European Cup-winning season saw him replace David Herd in the club's forward line. He remained at Old Trafford where he won two England caps and was then transferred to Arsenal in 1974 for £110,000. Eventually he went into coaching and was assistant to Sir Alex Ferguson at Old Trafford at one point.

George Best restores United's lead against Benfica.

Looking back on the European Cup triumph, Bobby Charlton said: "The win against Benfica in extra-time was a case of overcoming them with our stamina and our will to win. A lot of people don't appreciate how important the will to succeed was. If you have the will anything is possible and, on the night, that is what we had. Once we had won against Real Madrid in the semi-final, I thought it was fated that we would win the European Cup. It was our destiny."

He remembers the night being hot, and dehydration being a problem in the days before people stood on the touchline handing out water bottles to overheated footballers.

"In the evening I was so ill with dehydration that I kept fainting when I tried to get out of the hotel bed to go the official function. I stayed upstairs. Nowadays, after the game I would have been given the right things to eat and drink and would be prepared properly, but then it was just a couple of bottles of beer or Coke after the game, and that was not the thing to do."

Albert Scanlon, who had been in at the start of Busby's European odyssey, was now in the stand at Wembley to see the culmination of that long and eventful journey. The

Bobby Charlton scores his team's fourth goal and the destination of the European Cup is beyond doubt.

Defiant Milburn makes it right

Matt Busby shares his joy and the European Cup with Pat Crerand and George Best.

match was exciting, but for Scanlon it brought back other memories as it was the first time he had seen Johnny Berry since the air crash, where the injuries Berry received ended his playing career. Sadly, he didn't recognise Scanlon, nor any of his former colleagues at Wembley to see the great day.

In his triumph Busby still had time for the players from another era. Jackie Blanchflower had asked Scanlon to get his programme signed for him by the boss. As Scanlon approached, a reporter shoved him aside and said he was trying to get an interview. Scanlon recalls: "Matt went ballistic and told the guy if he ever spoke to any of his players again like that he would never get another interview."

George Best and Bobby Charlton celebrate victory over Benfica.

Curiously Sadler recalls feeling a sense of anticlimax at the moment of Manchester United's greatest triumph. "It was a strange feeling. We had won and were Champions of Europe and we all went up and collected the Cup and our medals. All that we had been building for had been achieved and, in that moment, was now part of the past. The night before the game, I had told myself, whatever happened I should try to remember the game and now, in a flash, it was over and we were successful."

It was days later when the enormity of what had been achieved started to sink in and when he considered the long and tragic road the club and Busby had travelled since the 1950s to reach that night at Wembley. "I was playing alongside footballers who had survived the Munich crash and had been there at Wembley for the culmination of the crusade. As the days and weeks turn into months and years it is only then that you can look back and reflect how big that night was for the club and the team."

Having missed out on the 1963 Cup Final because his dad and his mates wanted to go drinking after the match, Kevin Smith was there for the game and it was a special night for his first trip to Wembley although he confesses the stadium itself was a disappointment and not as impressive as it appeared on television.

He said: "I travelled down with some mates and, given the players

David Sadler with the European Cup after his team's 4-1 victory.

Benfica had, I was not that confident. We'd come down on a coach and went straight to the ground to soak up the atmosphere. It was a big relief when we got to extra-time and then there was a huge relief when we scored soon after the restart. The confidence seemed to flow back into the team. It was a wonderful night but there was no time for celebrations after. It was back on the coach and home."

Peter Beetham had just turned 18 and, with a friend who had recently passed his driving test, travelled down to the match on a hot May day. The journey, he remembers, seemed to last for ever. They had tickets for the terrace behind the goal Stepney was defending in the second half. Their spirits soared as United took the lead but even then he was not totally confident and it came as no surprise when Benfica equalised.

He said: "The minutes were ticking down when Eusebio shot, and we could see the ball flying towards goal. It was as though, for a moment, time had stood still. It looked like a goal all the way and suddenly Stepney saved it. The relief on the terraces flooded over us. I could barely watch as we waited for the final whistle and extra-time. Then the goals started coming and there was this great sense of euphoria that we had won and were the first English club to lift the European Cup. By now it was dark and as Charlton lifted the trophy we could see the camera flash lights bouncing off it. That was a bit unreal.

"We stayed for the lap of honour, but then set off for home because it was work the next day and extra-time had already delayed us. We were both shattered by the whole event. As we drove back I could see brake lights coming on and thought the driver must have seen them but he hadn't and we ran into the back of the car in front. Luckily we were both unhurt and, although it made a mess of the car, that was soon forgotten in the light of winning the European Cup."

Bill Makin believes it was the team spirit that had been an integral part of United sides since the 1940s that had seen the European Cup lifted. He doesn't believe that the side which lifted the Cup was the best that United had produced since the war, but on the night the team played exceptionally well and the players all played for each other.

He recalls: "We had been confident of reaching the Final since the quarter-final stage. In fact we booked our coach then, we were so sure. In the days before motorways it was a long trip and we must have had the most ramshackled coach in the fleet, but it got us there.

I left work at 11am on the Wednesday morning and I was back the following morning. Here was no question of an overnight stay. I think some of our players put in performances like they had never produced before in their lives. It was an amazing match and a terrific night."

On their return to Manchester, Mike and Annette Kelly took their places outside the Town Hall to await the triumphal return of the team with the trophy. Annette recalls: "We had been at work on the morning of the match and then dashed down to Wembley. Suddenly we realised that we both felt absolutely exhausted and were falling asleep on the pavement. In the end we went home and watched the team on television. We both eat, sleep and live Manchester United and it had all been a fantastic experience."

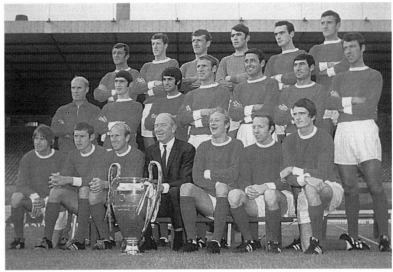

Manchester United with the European Cup in 1968.

One player missing the game was Denis Law. He watched the match from his hospital bed where he had undergone surgery on a knee. Yet even the absence of such a key figure had not prevented United fulfilling Busby's dream ten years after the disaster of the Munich air crash. Manager and players were now swept up in a tide of emotion. It was Manchester United's finest hour to that point.

The End of an Era

WITH the Holy Grail of the European Cup now achieved, one of the most successful eras in English football was coming to an end. Matt Busby would remain for one more season in the manager's chair, but his considerable shadow would make life difficult for his successors who struggled to emulate the triumphs of his reign.

Indeed, he would return briefly in the 1970-71 season following the decision to remove the man who replaced him, Wilf McGuinness. Yet his last full season in 1968-69 was not without its drama. Winning the European Cup ensured United would be back in Europe the next season and there was also a chance to take part in the World Club Championship against the South American champions, Estudiantes.

Conigliaro of Estudiantes (no. 9) sees his header saved by goalkeeper Alex Stepney during the second leg of the World Soccer Championship in October 1968. The game ended in a 1-1 draw but United lost 2-1 on aggregate.

The match against the Argentinians was memorable for all the wrong reasons. The famous *Daily Mirror* headline of the day summed it up succinctly when it declared the match was 'The Night They Spat On Sportsmanship', as the away fixture in Buenos Aires turned into a brutal battle. There was spitting, punching and crude tackles. Bobby Charlton needed stitches in his shin after one assault and Nobby Stiles suffered a cut over an eye following a butt. To add insult to injury United's combative midfielder was sent off in the closing minutes for disputing a decision with a linesman. It was only the second time he was sent off in his United career.

Stiles' reputation had unfairly gone before him. An uncompromising and, certainly, aggressive player, he was never the crude thug of popular legend and such a label did no justice to a player of considerable talent. The popular image of Stiles is the toothless man dancing around the Wembley pitch celebrating the England World Cup success in 1966. Yet his England success was complemented during a 14-year career at Old Trafford with two League Championship medals and a European Cup medal.

What helped cement his relationship with the fans was not just his on-the-field exploits, but the fact he had once stood on the terraces himself and cheered on the Reds. Playing for the team realised a childhood dream and his style of play meant he was always going to be a player the home fans adored, and the opposition supporters vilified.

One of the Argentinians' key players was Ramon Veron whose son, Juan Sebastian, is in Manchester United's midfield at the time of writing. It was a Veron corner headed home by Conigliaro that produced the only goal of the game. United thought they had scored an equaliser through David Sadler, only for the goal to be ruled out for offside. A decision Charlton still disputes to this day.

Busby was proud of the way his players had kept their cool despite such intense provocation and believed the tactics of the Argentinians had been disgraceful. In the return, United's cause was not helped when Veron scored an early goal and, against a side defending very well, the Reds struggled to get back in contention. George Best and Hugo Medina were sent off after a tussle. With three minutes remaining Willie Morgan scored to bring the scores level and Brian Kidd appeared to have netted the winning goal, only for the referee to claim he had blown for full-time. United were beaten, but the real damage was done to the reputation of the World Club Championship.

Bill Makin watched the Old Trafford tie and, even though it was in the days before organised football violence manifested itself, the crowd was so incensed by what was happening on the pitch they were prepared to vent their rage on a small party of Argentinian fans who were waving a huge national flag. "What their players were doing was so cynical it was unbelievable and I told the Argentinians to put the flag away and they came out with us after the game. It was just as well because there was a crowd waiting for them. It was out of character for United fans at that time, but that was how angry many were at what had happened in the game."

Manchester United still had their European Cup to defend and the draw handed them the simplest of opening rounds with the Irish side Waterford the opponents. A 3-1 win on Irish soil was followed up by a 7-1 victory at Old Trafford as United prepared for tougher opponents ahead. RSC Anderlecht were next up and a 3-0 win at Old

Trafford eased the pressure for the trip to Brussels. The Belgian side won 3-1 and, in a spirited contest, fought desperately for the fourth goal that would put them level on aggregate, but United held out.

On 14 January 1969, Busby announced that, at nearly 60, this would indeed be his last season as manager and the search should begin for his successor who would take over the reins at the beginning of the following season. His hope was that United would retain the European Cup so that his nearly 25 years at the club would end in triumph. First, though, the quarter-final opponents of Rapid Vienna needed to be overcome.

Denis Law is beaten to the ball by the Exeter City goalkeeper at St James's Park in January 1969 as George Best looks on. United won this FA Cup third-round tie 3-1.

Two days before the Rapid Vienna game, United had to play an FA Cup fifth-round replay against Birmingham City despite pleas to the Football Association for the match to be put back. It was not an ideal preparation yet the Birmingham game showed the Reds were on form as they won 6-2 with Denis Law scoring a hat-trick. When the Austrians arrived at Old Trafford they found United in irresistible form as the home side ran out 3-0 winners with Best netting twice and Willie Morgan scoring on his European debut.

By the time of the second leg United were out of the FA Cup having been beaten 1-0 by Everton. Also, it had not been an auspicious League campaign for United who were quickly off the pace. They won only 14 League games all season and perhaps the euphoria of the previous season had taken its toll. There was one outstanding result though with Queens Park Rangers beaten 8-1 in March and Morgan scoring the only League hat-trick of his United career. An eighth place finish was disappointing but there was still the chance as the season unfolded, that Europe would provide the setting for a glorious end to Busby's Old Trafford era.

A goalless draw in Vienna was enough to ensure a semi-final place against AC Milan.

For the first time supporters had the chance to watch the first leg in Milan on giant screens at Old Trafford and almost 23,000 turned up to watch the action in black and white. Over in Italy things were not going well as Milan took control of the game. Angelo Sormani scored the opener, which was allowed, despite protestations from United players that he had handled the ball. He had, though, taken advantage of some slack United defending. In the second half the home side doubled their lead through Kurt Hamrin. The United cause was further undermined when John Fitzpatrick was sent off for kicking Hamrin in an off-the-ball incident.

Busby believed the tie could still be won, but at Old Trafford the Italian defence were in parsimonious mood and their goalkeeper Fabio Cudicini (father of Chelsea's Carlo Cudicini) made a string of fine saves to deny United as they desperately pressed forward. It was the 70th minute before he was beaten when Best finally got clear of the markers who had hounded him and found Charlton, whose shot put United back in with a chance. Law appeared to have got the ball over the line for a second but the referee was having none of it and waved play on. It was the nearest United were to get and their European dream was over.

Busby praised his players for a magnificent effort and later waved farewell to the fans at the final League game of the season, a 3-2 victory over Leicester City at Old Trafford. One of the greatest managers in the history of the game had taken his bow, although he would remain at Old Trafford as general manager to work with his 31-year-old successor, Wilf McGuinness. In the early days McGuinness would concentrate on coaching, with Busby handling transfers, players' wages and the business side of being a manager.

John Fitzpatrick and Denis Law in action against Watford's Brian Garvey in the fourth round of the FA Cup in 1968-69.

David Sadler, who had been capped with Manchester United, would remain until 1973, when he moved to Preston for £25,000; he remained at Deepdale until injury ended his career in May 1977. He played 333 games for the Reds, but, looking back, believes the club failed to capitalise on the success achieved in the 1960s.

New United manager Wilf McGuinness addresses his new charges in the summer of 1969. But the shadow of Sir Matt Busby was always there.

He said: "1968 should have been the springboard to move on. The team contained older players just managing to get an extra bit out of their careers, with younger players now established and, in George Best, there was a player already recognised as one of the greats of world football. Yet rather than proving a springboard for the following years, winning the European Cup seemed almost like a stone around the neck of the club. Manchester United was to go into a fairly serious decline."

The pressures of trying to keep United at the top of the pack, coupled with a lifestyle of drink and beautiful women, meant that a player considered by many to be Manchester United's greatest, left Old Trafford in January 1974 after a disagreement with the then manager, Tommy Docherty. He played on for a while, but was a shadow of the player at his prime. His physical decline since then has been sad to witness.

Leicester City's Allan Clarke gets the better of Brian Kidd and Nobby Stiles in May 1969.

Best made his debut in September 1963 and is said to have described his initiation into top flight football as easy. Certainly, to those on the terraces, it seemed he had almost magical properties over the ball as he left defenders trailing in his wake. He was able to shine in a great team containing a host of leading players. His displays in the 1967-68 season culminating in the European Cup win saw him crowned European Player of the Year Award.

His fame and playboy lifestyle made him popular with the girls and he was one of the first footballers to attract the same attention as showbusiness stars, ensuring he was as likely to appear on the news and features sections of the papers as the sports pages. Busby had been a father figure and on his retirement the decline set in.

One young fan, though, has abiding memories of watching Best in his prime at Old Trafford. Roy Collins began taking his young daughter, Joan, to watch games at this time and she recalls: "I thought he was fantastic. I felt he was looking at me every time he glanced towards the Scoreboard End where we were."

Looking back on Busby's decision to retire Sadler says: "Matt was never a fit man when I knew him. That he had come back after surviving the crash and the injuries he suffered was an incredible achieve-ment. He was to carry the scars both physically and mentally for the rest of his life. Because he had been so strong mentally, he had been able to pick the club up and see them challenge in Europe. With the European Cup won, it was no surprise that he decided to call it a day. If there was a time to do it, I suppose it was then. With the benefit of looking back now, I think he had become very single-minded. By the end, I don't think there was any forward planning in place at all. All his efforts went on winning the European Cup with the team he estab-lished in the middle and late 1960s. 1968 was the culmination and his work was then done."

The Legacy and the Future

MANCHESTER United have become the world's richest football club and, during the 1990s and into the 21st century, one of the most successful as they have dominated domestic football perhaps even more so than their illustrious predecessors during the reign of Sir Matt Busby.

Under the charge of another soccer knight, Sir Alex Ferguson, the Red Devils have won seven Premiership titles, the FA Cup and Premiership double twice and, in their greatest season in 1999, they won the European Cup, Premiership and FA Cup in a thrilling treble.

Yet as the club passes its centenary mark, Ferguson for one recognises the importance of the history that Old Trafford is steeped in and the legacy he inherited. Fans too young to remember the great teams of the Busby era still sing out chants extolling Busby Babes. Many will have made their way to the ground along Sir Matt Busby Way. Others will have walked past the memorial to those who lost their lives at Munich.

At the time of the centenary celebrations, as he stood next to a player decked out in the kit of Newton Heath Football Club, which was the forerunner of Manchester United, Ferguson reflected: "We are always aware of history when we play. You can try to escape it but the past is a very important part of this club and I don't think there is ever a time when the players step out and they are not aware of that."

And he added: "At Manchester United people relate to the romance of the club. I am proud to have been given the chance to follow in Sir Matt's footsteps because it is his values and ideals which the club is created on. It's wonderful to be a part of it and I think it sums up what this club is about. There is tradition here, a way of playing, and I'm proud to be part of that legacy."

Others, though, have found the legacy of trying to emulate Busby a task too trying. In the years after Busby retired, David Sadler played under Wilf McGuinness and Frank O'Farrell, and saw the brief return of Busby himself before Sadler departed as Tommy Docherty arrived.

"Docherty saw the only way was to get rid of most of the old guard and start rebuilding from there. He had to go into the Second Division to do it, which happened with relegation in 1974. In 1968 we didn't think it would be long before we would be champions of Europe again. It turned out to be quite the opposite."

Sadler finds it hard to believe that it took a quarter of a century before Manchester United were again champions, and longer still before the European Cup was again back in the club's trophy room. "There were a lot of years after 1968 when things were not as they should have been at Old Trafford. After I finished playing, I stayed in Manchester and watched the team regularly, and it was not until the end of the 1980s and early 1990s when the necessary major changes took place."

Sadler is a great fan of the way the game has developed and believes it is now a marvellous spectacle. It helps, of course, that it has been a particularly successful time for his old club. And while the advent of big television money has boosted players' wages to incredible levels, he does not begrudge them their money. Since his playing days, and long before, he recognises there has long been an aura about the name Manchester United which remains to this day.

He reflects: "Why the club became what it is has been largely due to the work of Busby and Murphy. They were the major influences. It all started in the 1940s and early 1950s and was carried on, first by the Busby Babes and then by the 1960s side I played in. There has been a lull, but Sir Alex Ferguson has picked it up and brought the club to where it rightly belongs. I hope that success continues well into the new Millennium."

Just as players of a former era can barely contemplate the money their successors now earn, so the contrast between managers is just as great. Ferguson is reported to be on a deal worth £70,000 a week as part of a three-year contract. In 1963, Busby earned around £6,000 a year. Ferguson lives in a £1 million mansion in Cheshire, while Busby lived in a semi-detached house five miles from the ground.

If their lifestyles were different, with the current manager owning racehorses and his predecessor enjoying a round of golf on the local course, they have much in common in their philosophies as managers. The blend of producing young talent through the ranks, supplemented by big money signings is as much a Ferguson philosophy as it was for Busby. The philosophy of both was that United teams should play attractive, attacking football. Perhaps comparing lifestyles between now and 40 years ago is invidious. Certainly the fans are happy to watch the football.

Another to reflect that there is no comparison between the era he played in and today's game is John Doherty. He says that it is not just the style of football that has changed, but also the lifestyle of the players. "Today's footballers are more like film stars. One or two play like film stars. If I had my time again, I wouldn't change a thing even though I was injured and my career was over at 23."

Training is obviously more scientific than in Doherty's day, but he believes modern players overdo things. He jokes that he had never heard of torn hamstrings until the modern era. Certainly a regime of a gym workout and then a practice game, which was the norm when he played, did not put such a huge demand on players' bodies.

As for tactics, while there is a lot more focus nowadays, he still believes that football, at its heart, is a simple, straightforward game. Indeed, he thinks journalists and media pundits talk far more about tactics than do managers and players. "Journalists try to impress on people that they know something about the game by talking pretentiously about tactics, but most of them don't know much. If they did have a club, they wouldn't talk and write the drivel they do. It seems the last thing you need to be a football writer is any knowledge of football."

After they won the European Cup in 1968, John Doherty, like many others, expected Manchester United to build on that success, but it was not to be. It took the arrival of Alex Ferguson and the good fortune he had in keeping the job, even though he went five years without success, that has been the turning point for United. The former Busby Babe still likes to watch and, like others packed into the 'Theatre of Dreams', he finds the recent triumphs of the club unbelievable.

He explains: "I enjoy modern football but I don't buy into the views of Sky Television that every match is magnificent, wonderful. I see some good games, some okay games and some poor games, but I guess I'm not trying to sell their programmes. Some of the modern players don't give credit to the old sides. Peter Schmeichel was silly to say that the United team he played in could have given the Babes a ten-goal start. Denis Law joked, of course, that they could because we're all in our 60s now. To try to compare across the eras is impossible. All I know is that the squad of players at United pre-Munich was as good as any squad the club has had in its history."

Doherty believes there is an aura about Manchester United now that, love them or loathe them, commands admiration and respect. And, although the club is big enough to survive any downturns in football finances, he thinks others will not be so lucky. Yet some things don't change. In his day, fans always thought they knew more than the manager about the game and the best team to put out. It is the same today, he says.

Johnny Morris still watches Manchester United games occasionally but has to confess he finds the modern game boring. As he sees it, 20 players are all crammed into a quarter of the field one minute and the next they are all crowded into another quarter of the field. And given the amounts modern footballers earn, the man who turned his back on Old Trafford over a £750 benefit has no regrets. "I don't envy modern players their money. I hope they are enjoying it. We played when we weren't on big money, but we enjoyed it."

Modern players also get a better deal. He recalls an anecdote that shows how weak the position of professional footballers was in their dealings with the clubs, even towards the end of his playing days. When he was at Leicester City, the manager held the view that by the time a player was 34, he was finished.

As Morris takes up the story the manager was doing the rounds of the changing room. "He asked one or two of the players when they were born and I could see what was happening, so when he asked me I said 1924, which made me 33, and he wrote it down. There were three of us who gave a wrong age and we all got an extra 12 months playing. Many of the records still give my year of birth as 1924. It was 1923, but I wasn't going to tell him that."

The ex-players' association at Manchester United is also well organised, holds a series of events during the year and raises money for local charities. At such events Albert Scanlon gets the chance to reminisce with former colleagues. "There is a great friendship between all the lads who survived Munich. That includes Bobby Charlton. He is in a different world to us, as an ambassador for Manchester United and English football generally, but when he is with us, it is the Bobby Charlton we remember. He hasn't changed."

The club, despite its size and colossal wealth, has not lost sight of its grassroots. No more new supporters clubs can currently be created because the vast network in place already places too much demand on precious tickets. These clubs continue to enjoy a close affinity with the club and among each other.

At a pub in the Rossendale Valley in Lancashire, the local branch of the supporters club is holding one of its regular meetings, and it gives an insight into the way Manchester United keeps its grassroots support feeling part of the club, even though it is now a huge international concern. There is a link between this club in an East Lancashire valley and the Malta branch, who are some of the most ardent of United's international fans. The branch traditionally hosts travelling supporters and, on this night, there is a party over for a midweek match and the talk, of course, is of the Premiership.

The guest for the evening is Neville Neville, the father of United players Gary and Phil. He has brought a leather case containing a vast array of their medals, including, of course, the Champions League medals won by his sons in 1999. A steady queue forms to gaze at the display. Phil Neville is the branch's honorary president and regularly attends functions. Variations on such scenes will be repeated at other branches on other nights. It is the fact that, as far as possible, Manchester United does not lose touch with the ordinary fans that has kept the club a success, even in the years when silverware eluded them.

The last word goes to the player who has done so much for Manchester United and football in this country. Sir Bobby Charlton believes the Busby legacy still lives on, and there is still an expectation that the club must provide something special on the football field as it did in the days of Busby and the Babes. The history of exciting, crowd-pleasing players has been continued in the decades since Busby stepped down from the manager's chair. Players that express themselves and excite the public, like David Beckham, Ryan Giggs and Ruud Van Nistelrooy, are continuing in the tradition.

As the Old Trafford legend says: "Manchester United is still the Manchester United that Matt Busby dreamed of. It is a club looking forward, while aware of its past, and continuing a tradition of playing football that first and foremost entertains the public who pay to watch. The club continues in his tradition and is in safe hands."